YOU GET WHAT YOU GIVE

Merlin U Ward

Copyright © 2013 by Merlin U Ward

All rights reserved. In accordance with the US Copyright Act of 1976, the scanning, uploading, and electronic scanning of any part of this book without the permission of the publisher and author is unlawful piracy and theft of the author's intellectual property. If you would like to use material from this book (other than for review purposes), prior written permission must be obtained by contacting the author directly at muw@MerlinUWard.com.

Thank you for your support of this author's rights.

Acknowledgements

My wife
You will always be my #1 even when I'm up late working, writing or brewing. Thank you for putting up with me.
I love you.

My mentors
Thank you for giving me the guidance and kick in the pants needed to get me where I am today. I am forever grateful.

Renegades
One of the best groups of people with which I have had the pleasure of working. Thank you for giving me the opportunity to be a part of the team. Looking forward to all that is to come!

SMUN, UsGuys, BRANDidos, Community Managers & more...
It is you people that make the Internet so interesting. Continue striving to make it a better place for people and brands alike!

Table of Contents

PREFACE	1
START BY GIVING	4
GIVE TO GET BACK	7
DEFINE YOUR GOALS	8
METRICS	10
BUILDING BETTER HEALTH METRICS	11
BUSINESS METRICS GIVE YOU MORE	12
TRACKING ENGAGEMENT	15
CONTENT	17
WHERE TO FIND CONTENT	18
PUTTING CONTENT TO WORK	19
GOING VIRAL	21
CONSISTENCY AND THEMES	24
TARGETING SPECIAL INTERESTS	26
SOCIAL MEDIA POLICY AND GUIDELINES	30
WRITING YOUR POLICY: EMPLOYEES	31
WRITING YOUR POLICY: MANAGERS	32
SOCIAL MEDIA GUIDELINES	36
BASIC SOCIAL MEDIA STRATEGY	38

VALUES, CONTROVERSY AND LOVE	43
THE FIVE STRATEGIES	**47**
THE FOUR AUDIENCE METRICS	49
THE BRANDING STRATEGY	**52**
FAILURE TO LOCK DOWN	55
BUSINESS DECISIONS AND RACISM	59
PLACING YOUR BRAND	61
THE CUSTOMER SERVICE STRATEGY	**65**
THE POWER OF 'SORRY'	69
TRAVEL AND THE CUSTOMER SERVICE STRATEGY	74
TECH AND RESPONSE	79
FASHION STATEMENTS	81
THE COMMUNITY EXPERIENCE STRATEGY	**84**
MAKE THEM FEEL SPECIAL	88
JET BLUE AND COMMUNITY	91
A LESSON IN COMMUNITY	94
EMPOWERING EMPLOYEES	96
SEASONS FOR SUCCESS	99
THE INNOVATION STRATEGY	**103**
MASTER YOUR INDUSTRY	109
BEN & JERRY'S FLAVOR OF INNOVATION	111
CONTINUOUS INNOVATION	113
DO US A FLAVOR	115

THE INNOVATION GAME	117
THE SALES STRATEGY	**121**
A TIME AND PLACE	123
LEADING CONSUMERS TO BUY	125
FASHION SUCCESS	127
MORE THAN MONEY	128
REAL-TIME MARKETING	**133**
AUTOMATION	135
FINE-TUNING	**138**
MIXED STRATEGIES	140
MULTI-BRAND VS. SINGLE BRAND	142
PREPARING FOR TOMORROW	**145**
NOTE THE READER	**153**
ABOUT THE AUTHOR	**156**

Preface

It has been nine years since the launch of Facebook, seven years since the launch of Twitter and four years since marketers have seriously considered social media as a marketing channel. Online video and blogging have been around for more than a decade. However, it is still surprising that, in a world that creates more than 24 hours of video content every minute and more than 1 billion pieces of shared content a day, brands are still caught doing it wrong. Users generate millions of examples of effective social media behaviors every day, and while the marketers for major brands use social media well, they let their brands do it poorly.

The primary reason brands are flailing in this relatively new world is that they are breaking the rules of engagement. There is a big misunderstanding and ignorance by brands of how to communicate online with people — real people. Even though the people working in the company generally do it right with their personal profiles, brands misbehave.

You Get What You Give

There have been many books written on the basics of social media successes, best practices for social media, and how to drive success through targeted influencer marketing. Every social media conference you attend will ring the same three bells: listen, be present, engage. Another common refrain is the need for "transparency." Let's just call it what it is: being forthright and honest. All the books and conferences reinforce good behaviors for marketers, but those behaviors are the fundamentals. What those buzzword-laden conferences have yet to teach is how to grow your business.

This book is not about fundamental social media tactics, social footprints, big data, or influence. Those ideas and concepts are valid but they don't answer the overlying question — why?

This book focuses on "why." Why should you be on these networks? Why should your consumers care? Why are you investing your budget and time? We as marketers are quick to jump to the "what" and "where," but we are always late on answering "why." This book will explore the strategies that answer why you are on social media, give you ideas for building a process around your presence, and explain why your consumers should care, why you should want them to care more, and why you want them on your side.

The online landscape is moving quickly and the way consumers are using social media is rapidly evolving. Do not be

Preface

mistaken: Brands and people do not need to act very differently. Marketers spent all of 2006 promoting the goal of increasing followers and likes. This is a foolish practice that only measures the size of the ruler, not how it is used. Savvy marketers saw the flaws in this mindset and realized the future was in the relationships built through social media — yet they still spent the last three years promoting only one thing: engagement!

    Engagement generally correlates with the amount of output from your brand; however, engagement alone does not make your brand successful or make your business money! Engagement should never be your end goal with social media. Posting more, having more fans or followers, and getting more likes, comments or reach should also not be your end goals. They only tell you whether you are alive and thriving, or dying and being forgotten. If you are active on social media, then your social presence should be driving real business or campaign goals. Social media should be an integrated part of your business – something else this book intends to address.

Start by Giving

You do not need to already be using social media for this book to make sense, but you do need to buy into one philosophy before you read another page: Social media is about building relationships with the individual consumer. More importantly, those relationships take time to strengthen. The value of a strong relationship with even one consumer goes beyond any return on investment (ROI) formula you have been using in meetings or have read in a marketing book. You must understand that building an online presence will take time and there is no instant gratification.

You have to truly believe this.

We live in a customer-centric world where the consumers rule the marketplace. Millennial and Generation Z consumers' tastes jump quickly from one brand to the next with little regard for brand loyalty. There is also little room for stubborn brands that flood social streams with advertising messages. Even platforms themselves, like Facebook and Tumblr, see backlash from the people who use them daily when changes are made to make advertising more prominent in their networks. Marketing is revolving back to conversation, personal understanding and empathy for consumers. Call it what you want — after all, there are a lot of people building their brand on renaming this old idea. But the reality is you now not only have to know your consumers as individuals and cater to them as such, but you also need to have the technology to do so at a large scale.

It is upsetting to see brands abusing consumers and contributing to online noise. We as marketers and community managers need to go beyond the internal needs of our companies and fulfill the needs of the individual consumer. We can no longer lump consumers into broad categories. Messages that target broad categories do not connect and are often ignored. Consumers are demanding that we relate to their individual tastes, situations, and lifestyles, which means our audience matrices are becoming more complex.

Emotional and ideological factors now play a role in how we speak to our audience. For example, the self-proclaimed beer lover who purchases craft beer is different from the self-proclaimed beer lover who brews his own beer. Their level of passion toward beer is very different. While one consumes the end product and may recognize the differences in flavors from beer to beer, the other has a deeper understanding of how that beer was made, and what ingredients, processes and care go into creating those differences. It may seem subtle but the ideologies are different, which means the conversations are different in many ways. How you approach entertaining these two people varies, as well as how we should try to influence their purchase decisions. Their personal situations may also be different. All baseline demographics being the same, these individuals will still have different mindsets, life experiences and identities.

These factors all go into choosing the audience on which you want to focus your brand interactions online. You have primary and secondary audiences that use your product for different reasons. On top of this, each audience may be in different stages of purchase considerations. This all impacts how you should speak to individuals in your audience. While it may be overwhelming at first, consumers have a natural habit of ignoring content that doesn't pertain to them. You can use this to your advantage by speaking to your audience in micro-segments. You can speak to each of these micro-segments of your audience with content and messages to connect with them without being too disruptive of your overall audience. A good mix of content driven by insights on the individual micro-segments of your audience will ensure that you connect with individuals across all segments.

Building a presence online takes time, but every single individual you meet on the way counts. These nurtured relationships are the key to having longer and more profitable consumers. Good relationships with consumers make multiple areas of business easier for your brand, including customer service, advertising and sales.

Give to Get Back

Social media is a "you get what you give" ecosystem. You want more? Then you must give more. Giving more includes entertainment, education and even just good feelings. By researching your audience's interests outside of your products and brand, you can discover what makes them tick and what they have in common as a community. Your brand can use the findings of this research to help tie your community together and draw your audience closer to your brand.

If you ignore your audience's interests and only promote yourself, you will not get anything back. Your brand will earn a seat in the corner. While everyone else is sharing and helping each other find resources or entertainment, you will be alone and your brand ignored. Only the wallflowers that hover outside of the crowd might engage with you, and even then it may only be because you are in the way or inconveniencing them.

If you truly want to grow your presence on social media and begin driving your business toward better profits and increased brand awareness, you have to start by giving a little. Give your audience something that adds to their daily lives and you will get similar value back.

Define Your Goals

You must have an idea of what you want to achieve with your social presence. Behaving like you have already achieved your goals will give your brand presence a sense of confidence. If your milestone is to have 20,000 loyal followers, then you must act like you have 20,000 loyal followers and treat every follower you encounter on the way like a loyal follower. In this ecosystem, giving each and every follower the treatment you think a loyal follower should get will lead your followers to reciprocate that treatment – that's "you get what you give." Momentum will build (as long as you are consistent), and you will achieve your goals before you know it.

If you feel like you are talking to yourself because your brand is just starting out, it is likely that you really *are* talking to yourself. Keep in mind that no one wants to watch or read a commercial — people are always looking for ways to skip or opt out of commercials. Stop talking to yourself and try reaching out to people. Have a real human conversation as a brand. Ask a question that does not connect back to your products. This does not mean saying "Good Morning" every day or jumping on every single made-up holiday. Truly reach out to your consumers and learn about them.

Think of social media usage as being at a cocktail party; you are making the rounds. You have to wait for that right moment to jump into a conversation, and when you do, you make it count. Be interested in other people and you will become interesting. If you can make a difference in one person's life or even just give them something positive to think about, then you are doing it right.

Each strategy in this book uses a different type of content that drives a particular type of conversation and has its own risks and rewards. If you look at the list of strategies and think, "But how does this connect to sales?" then please stop reading and go reread the preface and this chapter.

Metrics

Your strategy boils down to what you want to accomplish with your brand. What is the outcome after you have found your audience, created an experience for them and added to, or become part of, their online behaviors? Your company has business goals and, at the end of the day, your online presence must be justified by the bottom line. Your goals will play a big role in which strategy you choose, but keep in mind the time it takes to do social media correctly. Your strategy may hinge on driving traffic to a specific online destination, moving the needle on any number of P&L indicators or driving incoming data needs.

No matter your business goal, your social metrics must be tied to it and must be measurable. There is a lot of debate surrounding what constitutes good social media metrics, but they can be broken into two categories: "health metrics" and "business metrics."

Building Better Health Metrics

Health metrics are sometimes referred to as "vanity metrics," but that is honestly too harsh of a term. These metrics are important, but are easier to fudge. Health metrics describe any activities that measure how your presence touches your audience and how it was received. These metrics are a part of the Four Audience Metrics (explained later) and include the following:

- Followers/Fans/Subscribers: the sheer number of people following your brand on a network.

- Views/Reach/Impressions: the number of times your content has been seen by your audience.

- Engagement: the number of times users have taken action on your content, which could be in the form of likes, comments, shares, retweets, repins, etc.

- Engagement rates: take the above engagement numbers and divide them by any of the following to get the rate of engagement: followers/fans/subscribers, number of posts, or period of time.

- Sentiment: the overall mood toward your content.

These metrics only tell you how many people might have seen your content and, in general terms, how much they might like it or dislike it. Knowing that 10% of your audience clicks "like" on your Facebook content is a helpful benchmark. These can be useful metrics, but do they support your goals? Depending on the size of your business, you, your boss, or your shareholders are expecting a return on the business output. Reaching a milestone in the number of followers does not mean you have a strong business or are making profits. None of the above measurements can be attributed to dollars on the bottom line.

The big issues with those metrics is that they miss a key denominator — the need to connect with the real person behind that "like" and the actions that customer takes that put money in your bank. You can attribute improvement of your business numbers to the actions that people take with your content, but it requires setting up the process before you begin. The ways brands can track these metrics and their attribution is getting better every day.

Business Metrics Give You More

There are better ways to measure social media, and brands need to start using them. You should know how much engaged people are contributing to your goal, whether that be dollars, pieces of information, brand recognition, number of referrals, number of entries or purchase intent. Track the actions your audience takes that lead to your end goal and which content was responsible for making that action happen. These are business metrics.

It is much more valuable to know information like:

John Doe, an avid follower of your brand, buys $50 of product from your website three times a month. He also comments on your content an average of five times a month. When he sees a specific type of content, he usually clicks on the attached link.

Once you cross-reference your purchase data with your social interactions, you can find people like John Doe and better develop your relationship with them. Additionally, you can create models around these individuals to create your micro-segments. You may find that people who behave like John Doe are also 25% more likely to buy $50 of product from your website.

This is not impossible data to compile. It just requires forethought in developing a process that allows you to cross-reference your point of purchase data and survey data with your engagement and follower data.

You should also catalog your content incessantly, even if you have to do it manually. This will help you attribute meaningful actions with results. Each post, its copy and imagery, should be logged and have meta data attached to it. Comparing the engagement rate of individuals with your purchase database will give you great insights to your audience's behaviors throughout the purchase life cycle. For instance, you may find that a person who follows you on Twitter *and* is a Facebook fan, and likes or retweets your posts once a week, is 50% more likely to make her first purchase than someone who is *only* a Facebook fan. The question then is "why?" and the answer may simply be that she is exposed to a better mix of messaging. If that were the case, then you would want to mix more messaging from both channels or encourage your Facebook fans to also follow you on Twitter.

Do not be fooled by big numbers of likes or followers. Social media is a relationship game, not a numbers game. Once people develop a relationship with your brand, they are much more likely to respond to your call to action. Compare these kinds of engaged followers to the tens of thousands of people force-fed content that resembles ad copy for "brand x" and have made a habit of ignoring that brand. The people you engage with the most are more receptive and relatively easy to track, and there are many other people who do not engage as often that you can still target.

Some of these people may feel like they have a relationship with your brand just by seeing your content regularly, even if they do not engage often. If you are properly tracking your content and engagements, you can identify these stealthy, sporadic engagers and develop deeper relationships with them through content they enjoy.

Tracking Engagement

There are a number of ways you can track interactions with fans. One is to track their activities manually. Most social networks give you the names of people who engage with your content. Keep these names in a database or spreadsheet and continually update and amend that data with other business metrics you have.

Another way to track social interactions is to use software tailored to this purpose. Many companies use Customer Relationship Management (CRM) software to keep track of their customers' emails and purchase patterns. Social media, in a similar way, houses a large of amount of personal information that people willingly offer up to social sites. The challenge over the last few years has been marrying the social media with CRM databases. Many software companies are getting very close. Tools like Salesforce, Adobe Social and Nimble all have integration of traditional CRM with social analytics and additional analytics, including website behavior, specific point or purchase data, and digital advertising. With these tools, you can track individuals, segments and broad audiences to identify

You Get What You Give

trends among their behaviors on social media, your website and purchases. The price point of these services varies, but I encourage you take the time to explore this kind of software.

Content

Your brand's voice must be apparent in your content. Social media is one of the few places where you can tell your story in real time. Your stream of content sets a course for how your audience will engage with your brand down the road.

In other words, your content tells a story. Your story should continue long after the 30-second video clip someone watched; it continues throughout all your posts. It evolves and is retold by your audience. The best story is one that your audience can relate to, participate in and translate into their own words. This story does not need to be complex. Simple is better, and personal stories are best. When your audience feels involved in your story, they can share it as if it were their own. When they feel like they own it, they will also value it and protect it. I promise your consumers who appreciate your story will feed your bottom line.

Where To Find Content

The content you use to tell your story can come from a variety of sources. First, you can have your creative department make your own branded content. This type of content gives you the most control over your message; however, it also has the highest chance of resembling advertising. Professionally developed content must be carefully crafted to fit within the platforms you choose so that it does not look "canned" and get lost in the advertising clutter. You need to strike a careful balance between being noticed and being noisy. Having imperfections can be to your advantage, as your content will blend better with other content your audience sees from its friends. It makes your brand seem more human and less like a corporate robot.

Another content option is memes. "A meme is an idea, style or action which spreads, often as mimicry, from person to person via the Internet, as with imitating the concept... An Internet meme may take the form of an image, hyperlink, video, picture, website, or a hashtag. It may be just a word or phrase."[1] New memes are created almost weekly and popular memes will rise to the top as your audience shares them. Be mindful that a meme that is popular on the Internet may not be popular among or known by your audience, or be a good fit for your brand. Use memes with caution and, when possible, research whether your audience is using them.

The last source for content is your audience itself. You have an especially great opportunity if your product or service has a unique experience built into it. Consider all the videos on the Internet of cats riding a Roomba. That is user-generated content and could be used in a variety of ways by the Roomba brand.

You may find that some of your audience is already creating their own content around their experiences with your brand. If you share their content and ask the rest of your audience to follow suit, your brand could have its very own meme on its hands. Staying on top of current events, both online and offline will help you keep the best content in front of your audiences.

Putting Content to Work

Develop a full calendar of available content you already have at your disposal and use that content to map out your story. The calendar should include any content that supports your strategy and the "why" for that channel. It should closely resemble an editorial calendar, with the addition of story arcs that support your brand story. Just remember: The content should fill a need for your audience.

You Get What You Give

You can optimize your content using the engagement "health metrics." The amount of engagement you get on the types of content you distribute should give you insight into what helps your brand connect best with your audience. The type of content that achieves the most attention should be used more often, with variances in messaging and conversation tactics. Be mindful that, as a collective, your audience's reactions may vary based on the size of the micro-segment and sometimes the time of year. Watch carefully which individuals respond most often to each type of content you post and how they respond. Most importantly, be sure the actions individuals take support your "business metrics."

You can incorporate nearly unlimited types of content into your strategies. You can use video, images, infographics, graphs, text, games and more. No matter what content you choose, it is important that you keep your brand identity constant in all these forms. This includes your voice, tone and brand values. Content, shared or created, should abide by your policy on the use of sex appeal, sarcasm, controversy and humor. Consistency in your brand, across all the marketing elements and content, will help maintain your audience's expectations on each platform.

Going Viral

Your content is your vehicle for creating real connections with your audience. A good piece of content does not need to go viral. Viral content isn't always good content, nor does it always reflect your brand. Your goal should not be to create the next viral video or most-shared meme on the Internet. As nice as it would be to have an explosive amount of impressions on your creative content, it should not be the gauge for your success. Content that impacts your community is always good content. Your goal should be to engage your audience with meaningful content, not pizzazz, to build trust with them.

If you happen to have a piece of content go viral, then congratulations! However, one popular piece of content does not mean you have made it. Your work has just begun. Your first challenge will be determining the cause of your viral content. Was your content virality a fluke or a direct effect of something you did? You must isolate the spark that caused the fire.

There are really only two ways your content can go viral:

1. It was shared by an influential person
2. A community of people shared it enough that it caught on outside of that community.

You Get What You Give

Somewhere down the line, someone or some group of people shared your content and brought people to view and engage with it. Once you find that original person or people, you must find out why they decided to share it.

One extreme example would be that a prominent profile with an active following, such as well-known news organization or a celebrity, shared your content, which gave it instant credibility in front of thousands or millions of people. The other extreme would be that a group of individuals shared your content, which set off a chain reaction within that community, which caused it to spread to a wider audience. Those communities then continued to shared your content over and over again until the general public became aware of it.

Both ways make your content viral, but one puts more weight on whether the content itself connected with people and was the cause of your viral success. If it was the latter, you have good grounds to continue to create similar content in hopes that these people will continue to share. If it was a well-known person or profile, then you may not be able to replicate your viral status – and you may not want to.

Do not let the exception become the rule. If your content went viral because a single profile shared it, the content itself may not be why it was so popular. The people who engaged with it may be taking those actions only because it was shared by someone they like, rather than because the content intrigued them. There will be many people outside of your immediate audience engaging with your content, but you must be sure that your audience also engaged with it and enjoyed it. Because you are diligently tracking your content, followers and engagement, this should be easy to figure out.

In either scenario, your challenge will be to define whom the new people who engaged with your content are and why they may have followed your account. Viral content often comes with an influx of new followers. Depending on how your content was pushed across the Internet, people may follow your account for reasons you did not intend. Try to get an understanding of your new audience members and determine if they are really interested in your brand or in that one piece of content.

During the big NFL game in 2013, Oreo put out a piece of content that went viral during the now-infamous blackout. While the audience waited for half an hour for the game to come back, Oreo tweeted, "You can still dunk in the dark."[2] Not everyone can pull off the Oreo "Dunk in the Dark" post. That post was highly effective and spoke to millions in a timely and relevant way. Strip away the circumstance and you still have a brand that knew how to connect with its audience using its brand's voice. The content went viral because of a perfect mix of the right opportunity and well-developed content that spoke to the Oreo audience.

You Get What You Give

What many marketers failed to realize was that there were many other brands that made equally meaningful posts for their audiences during the blackout. Audi, Walgreens, PBS and even Tide created timely content that received significant attention by their audiences.[3] These brands' tweets received engagement that any brand or agency would have loved to have, but alas, all the marketing hot sheets the next day covered the beloved Oreo.

Consistency and Themes

Oreo was also doing something else that worked in their favor. Even before the big game, Oreo had spent time posting to its audience on a regular basis. The key to the success of your content and ultimately your platform presence is consistency. You need to be *consistently* creating content. For this book, "consistently" is defined as posting thematic content at least once a week, if not daily. No matter which networks you choose to participate in, make sure you are equipped to participate consistently.

It is arguably more important that your brand creates content with a consistent theme than that you do it in a timely way. This is especially true for networks that use visual content. Your brand should produce a series of content that works together, rather than an eclectic collection. This has been proven time and time again on networks such as Instagram and Vine. Any user with more than 10,000 followers has been producing content with a consistent theme regularly.

For example, consider Khoa Phan on Vine. His six-second stop-motion videos featuring paper cutouts intrigued a community. Or look to Murad Osmann on Instagram, who has a hashtag image series under #FollowMeTo. He takes pictures of his girlfriend pulling him along to some of the most popular travel destinations in the world. Photographers and travelers alike follow him and his work. Both have earned national attention in a relatively short period of time and both had fewer than 200 pieces of content on their respective accounts when they earned that media boost. They both have successfully found their voice with an audience that appreciates their work, and the same is possible for brands.

During the big game, Oreo also launched its "Cookie versus Cream" campaign on Instagram. The premise of the campaign was that consumers had a favorite part of the famous cookie — either the cream or chocolate cookie — and they would battle to the death over which was better. To celebrate this friendly "death match," Oreo posted images of sculptures made entirely from the cream or the cookie parts of an Oreo, using photos submitted by users as direct inspiration. For three days, Oreo posted a number of new images on Instagram that fit this series, generating more than 35,000 followers. Once that series was complete, the brand moved on to the next series under the same campaign, this time using cookie and cream separator machines.

Oreo generated spurts of themed content for a number of days and, in five months' time, attracted more than 85,000 followers with fewer than 200 pieces of content.

Sharpie has also harnessed the power of consistency and thematic content on Instagram. Although the brand joined Instagram in December 2010, the brand's series of content didn't begin until March 2012. This is when Sharpie finally found its voice by creating unique drawings made purely from Sharpie's selection of colorful markers. In a period of three months, it successfully tripled its engagement on the platform and accelerated its fan growth, creating a healthy presence. Now with just over 300 pieces of content, it has more than 85,000 followers. Unlike Oreo, Sharpie manages to post multiple times a week. The company has kept a consistent level of engagement throughout, with roughly 10% of its following interacting with the brand at any given time.

Targeting Special Interests

Supporting special interests through content is a sensitive subject for brands, but is also a great way to connect with the audience's emotions. Content plays a huge role in brands' contributions to causes such as gay rights, women's rights, access to health care, and racial equality. It is part of Internet culture for your audience to share and support causes as it sees fit. Showing support for special interests and in disaster situations provides opportunities for your brand to connect with your audience in incredible ways, but it must be done earnestly. Pursuing this type of content distribution will put your policies and brand to the ultimate test. How you decide which causes to support should be left for internal discussion.

For example, on March 26, 2013, the U.S. Supreme Court began hearings for equal marriage rights for homosexual couples. Many Facebook users adopted a red equal sign in place of their profile pictures to show their support for the movement. It was not long until users generated memes of the symbolic sign, including *Star Wars* and bacon-themed images. Individuals were not alone in their meme creations. Brands also contributed to the cause and spread awareness to millions of their audiences across Facebook. Martha Stewart, the *True Blood* TV show, Smirnoff, Bud Light, Absolut, Bonobos and Kenneth Cole each created content in support of equal marriage rights. As of May 2013, Barkbox still had its Facebook brand page image set to a doggie variation of the equal sign.

Showing an inkling of human emotion and empathy can go a long way with your audience. People are quick to turn away from a brand and create PR storms online when brands do not support causes, and many brands are forced by the masses to change their ways. Stay on top of how your audience feels about specific current events and you will keep your brand out of the news for the wrong reasons.

You are mistaken if you think your consumers cannot break your brand. Their view of your brand is the primary reason your brand has meaning and value. Without your consumers' support, your brand will be forgotten. We now live in a world where the consumer has a small voice and where a small voice can quickly turn into a mob. That mob can quickly tarnish your brand and sway the opinions of bystanders. In the next few pages, you'll read how strategy and the supporting tactics can work in your best interest or take a turn for the worst. Some of the mistakes that follow seem like obvious mistakes in hindsight, but the teams that created the campaigns thought they were grand ideas. Before pursuing any content, first consider what your audience will think.

Your content is more than just the opportunity to go viral. It is the medium for your brand message, and your brand should tell a story that has meaning to your consumers, not just the brand. A story typically has three parts: a beginning, middle and an end. It can build anticipation and suspense or make a person smile. Tell your story and get your audience to participate in the story. If you feel especially adventurous, give your audience the opportunity to write a part of the story. A trusting brand earns the trust and support of its fans quickly.

Endnotes

1 Wikipedia, "Internet Meme." Accessed October 20, 2013. en.wikipedia.org/wiki/Internet_meme.

2 Huffington Post, "Oreo's Super Bowl Tweet: 'You Can Still Dunk in the Dark.'" Feb. 04, 2013.
http://www.huffingtonpost.com/2013/02/04/oreos-super-bowl-tweet-dunk-dark_n_2615333.html.

3 McGee, Matt. Marketing Land, "Oreo, Audi & Walgreens Newsjack Super Bowl "Blackout Bowl."" Feb. 03, 2013.
http://marketingland.com/oreo-audi-walgreens-market-quickly-during-super-bowl-blackout-32407.

Social Media Policy and Guidelines

Before you even begin to consider a social media strategy, you must first give your company a playbook. A well-thought-out policy of what to post and what not to post when responding to your audience will save your brand a lot of worry and headache. Your policy objective is to outline every possible scenario you might encounter with your audience within reason. Work with your social media team to determine how these scenarios will be handled. Your team knows more about social media and how people engage online, but the brand must come first, and its values must be protected.

There are no templates for a social media policy. It all depends on your company values, your team's abilities and the amount of responsibility you want to give that team. One policy will not work for every kind of company. You can view other brands' policies, but ultimately your policies will be uniquely your own, tailored to your company and your messaging.

Writing Your Policy: Employees

Your social media policy will be relevant for two groups of people: Employees and managers. Employees can play a crucial role in your online presence and, when empowered to participate, can prove to be a valuable resource. But just like any resource, they must be properly managed. The guidelines for employees should have three areas of consideration: conduct, content and disclosure.

The first part, conduct, outlines how you expect your employees to behave online and on the brand's social media properties. It is not a far stretch to ask your employees to stick to your brand's values when they discuss your brand with other people, especially where the brand is visible, such as on your Facebook page. Try not to view this as governance. Present this to your employees as an opportunity to support the company for which they work and love. Approach this section of your policy as a list of encouraged behaviors as opposed to "things not to do." Empowering your employees to be active on social media, for themselves and for the company, can be a major benefit to your organization. Having one hundred people, or even a handful, to speak for your brand will give you a lot of leverage, especially when there is news to share.

The second part of an employee policy is content. This part of the policy outlines what kind of content your employees can share when talking about the brand, as well as where to find company content to share. Some companies have gone so far as creating a space where employees who are content creators are highlighted on the company website. Aggregating employee content, company content and third-party content for your entire staff to share will make you a formidable force in the social media realm.

Last in the employee policy is disclosure. Employees should always disclose that they are a part of your company. This is especially important when engaging with your audience. It is even more important if your company is in a regulated industry. This creates accountability for your employees, and also enables you to hold them responsible for their actions.

Writing Your Policy: Managers

The second part of your policy is for your social media managers or community managers. The first item for consideration is how to handle complaints. No one complaining about your brand should be ignored; all direct mentions of your brand – those that use your brand's handle specifically – should be answered. Some complaints may be blunt or brash and require finesse. Some situations may require a more politician-like style. In other situations, crystal-clear communication will be best.

While you should engage with these complainers, ultimately you want to avoid a shouting match or argument. Often people just want to know they are being heard. It is best that you manage these situations publicly, if possible. By addressing concerns publicly, you create the opportunity to resolve issues with other consumers who may have felt the same way but did not speak up (many do not).

The second item for consideration is how to deal with questions. You will encounter a number of inquiries from people online and you should be prepared to respond to as many as possible. Some will be day-to-day questions you are already familiar with and others may seem very strange. This is your opportunity to truly engage and show that you're listening to your consumers.

Take this opportunity to learn about your consumers and where they are from. The trigger for their question is likely to be tied to a situation affecting their lives, such as their financial situation, social situation, family dynamics, or simply where they are located. Through a natural conversation, you can discover more about them and why their questions are occurring. Their situations may be unique, but your insights may help that customer or others later, so keep track of the information you learn.

Basic questions may have easy answers and others may need to be vetted by your lawyer. For the day-to-day questions, you can create documents that explain answers to these questions in more detail than the given platform may permit, so that if all else fails, you can point your audience to these documents through links. You can even make your answers entertaining — just another opportunity to add to your consumer experience.

The main concern of your social media policy for managers will be public attacks. Your PR protocols for handling crises offline are likely not suitable for social media. In 2013, Nutella was caught sending a cease-and-desist letter to an American blogger, Sara Rosso, for creating "World Nutella Day."[1] She developed the idea in 2007 as a way to celebrate her favorite condiment. The legal department saw "World Nutella Day" as an attack on the brand and had been sending Russo cease-and-desist letters for six years. Needless to say, the online community was outraged and fans were shocked that Nutella would sic their lawyers on an outspoken fan. Nutella eventually issued a statement that their CEO had contacted Rosso and signed off on the holiday. This was chalked up as a misunderstanding, but it is a clear example of how the normal routes of dealing with "attackers" may not be the best.

So what do you do when someone really attacks your brand? Depending on the situation, you may want to just acknowledge the person and let them know you have heard them. Other attacks may be an opportunity to publicly educate your audience.

Ignoring an attack is rarely the correct approach. You must respond. This is an opportunity to educate your audience about your product. Don't miss it!

Do not leave your social media team lingering in difficult situations. Make sure you have an outlined protocol on how to handle each level and type of attack on every platform. Give your team the freedom and guidance to handle the minor attacks, while getting advisement on more serious attacks. It is bad policy to escalate all attacks to supervisors, which can become time-consuming and create more frustration for your attacker. Avoiding PR pitfalls is the ultimate goal of your social media policy.

For every strategy, you must attempt to prepare answers to all questions before they are posed and have a plan for every possible audience reaction that could occur. It is said a good plan is nothing without action. Having a plan of action will save you a lot of time and stress. Plan ahead to put out fires, small and large. Social media is a fast-moving world and situations can be

You Get What You Give

quickly forgotten, but they can also be dragged up again if no attempt to fix them was made.

Your policy should enable your team to answer all potential questions in a timely manner. A good policy will outline every reasonably imaginable scenario and include guidance on how to handle them. Many of them may be handled in similar ways. Nevertheless, expect that you will still encounter surprises.

Social Media Guidelines

Social media guidelines are for your audience and explain your expectations of good conduct on your channels. Many of your channels are left open for your audience to voice their opinions. Your blog, Tumblr, Facebook and YouTube account, just to name a few, all have places for your audience to post comments. Your guidelines should explain the rules of engagement to which the individuals in your audience will be held. The guidelines are the ground rules of your channels. Major brands like Coca-Cola, Burger King and Target all have some form of guideline posted publicly. Each channel may have different rules, but overall, these guidelines are there to help your audience engage with you and each other.

Your guidelines should also include the actions that will be taken against people who do not abide by them. The Internet is huge and you will encounter personalities of every type. You will also encounter a variety of ideals, belief systems and points of view from around the world. You will see racism, hate, slander and derogatory statements. Although the Internet is a place of free speech, your brand does not need to be tarnished by the opinions of others or by inappropriate or unrelated comments.

Your guidelines should include your right to delete any kind of disrespectful behavior and give your team the power to take action on any channel. Post your guidelines in easy-to-find areas and link to them on the landing pages and bios of your brand. Make sure they are well-known and enforceable.

Endnotes

1 Quan, Kristene. TIME, "'World Nutella Day' to Cease and Desist." May 21, 2013. http://newsfeed.time.com/2013/05/21/world-nutella-day-to-cease-and-desist/.

Basic Social Media Strategy

Why do your consumers care? Or rather, why should they? When it comes to brands, consumers have options. A lot of options. You have competitors and, in many ways, you aren't very different from them. You have similar products and may even have the same quality of customer service or prices. Your mission and the purpose of your marketing is to set you apart from your competitors. The goal is to create a unique experience that differs from any of your competitors and positions your brand where it can control the message or drive your audience to control the message. That is fundamental, and that is where strategy begins.

Basic Social Media Strategy

Each channel can play a different role in your social media marketing. Think of it as your home: Each room has a purpose. Your living room has a TV and it's the place where you relax. Your kitchen has a fridge, oven and microwave, and that is where you prepare food. Your bathroom has a toilet with its very own special purpose. You walk into those rooms knowing what you want to do and, for the most part, know what to expect when you get there. Your online channels are like that house — your consumers are moving from room to room. The key to a successful marketing strategy is building the right expectations of the brand and fulfilling those expectations for the audience in each room.

Consider all the marketing elements you have in your repertoire. You have a website, Facebook page, Twitter account, YouTube channel, blog and other more niche channels at your disposal. Each of those platforms is like a room in your home. Each room in your marketing home has its own offerings and comes with its own expectations. Your job as the brand is to answer for the audience, "Why should I go there?"

Most brands have no idea why people go to their channels. They just keep pumping out content, expecting a return. Understanding the purpose of each room and the amenities (or assets) for each and how they are used is crucial when it comes your customer experience. Build your home carefully and with purpose, and people will actually want to spend time in it! Be aware that once people move into that house, they may be inclined to remodel. Even though you built different rooms for different purposes, the inhabitants may want to move the furniture around or use a room for an entirely new purpose. One room may be built under the Branding Strategy, but your audience wants Customer Service. In this case, you should go with the flow instead of sticking to the original plan.

The latest statistics say that, on average, 40% of people follow a brand for the chance to collect a special offer or coupon.[1] One-third of an audience follows a brand because it's comprised of existing customers. Meanwhile, 20% follow your brand for interesting or entertaining content. The remaining 7% of your audience follows your brand for a range of reasons, from customer service to a recommendation from a friend. These statistics are just generalizations, and the truth is your exact statistics are unique to your company.

In early 2013, freight company UPS and comScore released a joint study on retail brands on social media. They found that 60% of retail followers followed purely for coupon opportunities. The next group, at 47%, also liked the retailer's Facebook page only because that action had been incentivized.

This example makes it clear that your social media presence is unique and so are your audience's reasons for following you. People will initially follow your brand for any of the aforementioned reasons, especially if they are incentivized, but

Basic Social Media Strategy

the success of your strategy and your social presence rests on what you do with those followers once you have them. First and foremost, your approach to growing your audience should fit your strategy. They may start following your brand because you dangled the proverbial carrot, but once they bite, you still need to seize the opportunity to connect with them on a deeper level. You should offer reasons to come back and continue to engage with your brand and help you spread your brand to the farthest corners of the Internet and beyond.

To kick off its Facebook page, the Kraft Foods condiment brand Grey Poupon created a Facebook application that asked one simple question: "Do you have good enough taste to 'Like' Grey Poupon?" With permission, the application accessed the person's profile information and examined a range of interests and statistics about their Facebook presence to give them a chance to "like" the page and join the "Great Taste Society," as they called it.[2] In a clever and interactive way, the application rated a person's profile, highlighting information it discovered during the examination process, such as how many likes they received on posts, whether they used proper grammar and their tastes in music. In the end, each person received a score. If the score was high enough, the consumer was allowed to "like" the Grey Poupon page.

The application used its sarcastically highbrow brand voice and made a game of becoming a fan. The rejection notice for not passing the "test" read: "We are sorry, but your taste, like fine estate silver, could use a good polish." The process of being prequalified to "like" a page actually made people want to like it more. It gave people a unique sense of entitlement and ownership over their stake in the fan page presence. After being granted access (most people just needed to resubmit their profile for examination) the brand followed up with similarly clever content that set the tone for the rest of the relationship with the brand. It was funny and made people feel good.

The online world is driven by emotion. Once your audience begins to follow you, you as a brand are granted a window of time in which you can prove you are worth keeping in their feeds. After all, they have opted to let you become a part of their daily lives and trusted you to not abuse their bandwidth. Your posts will pop up on their feeds regularly. Your job is to trigger something inside your audience that makes them feel good and honors that trust. You must respect their willingness to let you show up on their feeds. Every time they check their phones while waiting in line or during commercial breaks while watching television, you will be there. Your strategy should position you to meet your goals by making your presence count and giving people content that resonates with them. Over time, they will reciprocate the value you bring.

Values, Controversy and Love

One thing that's of utmost importance to your audience is how much your values align with theirs. You do not have to please everyone, and the fanatics can be addressed as they come, but your brand should have a position on a number of issues like sex appeal, politics, and the use of humor and sarcasm. This is where your social media policy begins to drive your strategy. These values must be consistent in your brand across all the marketing elements and in the content used in your social channels. Your stance must also be strong. Sticking to your guns will eliminate mediocrity, and the audience that feels most aligned with you will support you all the way. Mediocre is honestly the worst perception your audience could have of your brand. It comes with zero enthusiasm and your engagement will suffer because you will fail to connect with people's emotions out of a fear of hurting someone's feelings.

Being controversial is also a tactic you might want to include as part of your strategy. Although a risky direction for some marketers, controversy at least comes with its fair share of publicity and supporters who will advocate for you.

In Ryan Holiday's book "Trust Me I'm Lying," you'll find this advice from Timothy Ferriss: "Study the top stories at Digg or MSN.com and you'll notice a pattern: the top stories all polarize people. If you make it threaten people's 3 Bs — behavior, belief or belongings — you get a huge virus-like dispersion." Holiday is the man behind the shock-and-awe campaigns for Tucker Max and American Apparel, and he guiltily mastered pushing the 3 B buttons. He discovered a still-thriving loophole in how the online PR machine works and used it to get controversial stories about his clients into major online publications. There is a lot of PR potential in polarizing an audience, and as the instigator, you cannot avoid being caught in the crossfire. There may be people on your side, but the real difficulty comes with all those who oppose your controversial stance.

Interestingly, being loved is just as difficult, and still requires a firm stance on a number of issues. Producing content that consistently generates feelings of joy, wonder, awe or triumph is challenging because you need to know what makes your audience tick. Just like you need to know how to get under people's skin when creating controversy, you need to know how to get in people's heads to make them feel good. To truly make them feel a connection with your brand — and not just with the image of the kitten you might have posted — requires that you have a deep understanding of your audience and what motivates them. That motivation is the tricky part, because while we all tend to get angry about the same things, we don't always experience feelings of joy about the same things. However, once you find that insight you can create a message that aligns with you audience. And the audience that aligns with your message of good feelings and kindness are more than likely the type of people who will also spread that message.

Whatever your brand's stance, it must be justifiable and not presented in a way that can be perceived as sheer arrogance. There is also no reason to be insensitive. Just because your stance opposes another person's point of view does not mean you need to treat them unjustly. (Although, remember: if controversy is the route you choose, there will be plenty of insensitive things thrown in your direction.)

You want to be as inclusive as possible with all the individuals within your audience. These majority and minority groups could be defined in a number of ways, which are completely up to you. Gender, location, interests, or even sexual preferences could define them. You want to be aware of all the emotions you evoke in each subset of your audience.

As said before, you can't always be a crowd-pleaser, but you still need variety in your content that connects with all your supporters. Lumping your audience members into broad categories puts you at risk of serving just the majority while ignoring the minority. Ignoring any group of supporters — even a small group — is a fast-track to rebellion against your brand. Everyone has a voice and their own audience in social media, and they will use them when they feel slighted or unappreciated.

You Get What You Give

Whenever possible, celebrate each subset of your audience with a special piece of content made just for them.

Your strategy should also be driven by a distinctive insight into how your audience behaves online. Before choosing the strategy, listen to your audiences and watch their behaviors on each network. Introducing a strategy with tactics that are unwelcome on any network will backfire quickly. Tactics that do not trigger the wanted response for the brand at the correct time will deflate your whole brand presence — just like jumping into the wrong part of a conversation at a cocktail party. You may find that you start with one strategy, but over time your consumers behave in a way that is best addressed under a different strategy — they remodeled your home! Your users may behave in a way better addressed with a different strategy from your original plan. Do not fight it. Just go with it! If they're asking for customer service on a platform you've set aside for something else, give them customer service. Don't swim against the grain if you catch the drift.

Endnotes

1 M, Azita. Get Satisfaction, "Infographic: What Makes People Want to Follow a Brand?." June 29, 2011.
http://blog.getsatisfaction.com/2011/06/29/what-makes-people-follow-brands/?view=socialstudies.

2 Hayden, Eric. TIME, "Are You Sophisticated Enough to 'Like' Grey Poupon on Facebook?." Sept. 17, 2012. http://newsfeed.time.com/2012/09/17/are-you-sophisticated-enough-to-like-grey-poupon-on-facebook/.

The Five Strategies

This book continues to explain concepts that have multiple moving parts and are based heavily on your company's internal processes and abilities. After reading this book, you will be able to create world-changing experiences for your consumers, whether you are a clever community manager, C-level executive or a member of a social media team. Before implementing a strategy, you must have goals, tactics for achieving those goals that you test constantly, and a willingness to try new things and participate in conversations with your followers. Your content will help drive this conversation and your metrics will help give you insights to the next steps. All the previous chapters were written to prepare you and build you up to this point.

The Five Strategies
1. **Branding**: driving brand value and recognition.
2. **Customer Service**: assisting customers online either with making purchases or with products to maintain brand reputation.
3. **Community Experience**: creating a community of people interested in your brand and communicating directly with that community.
4. **Innovation**: harness your brand's following to drive new products and services or improve existing products and services.
5. **Sales**: promote new products and increase product awareness amongst followers.

These strategies can assist a company of any size. Opportunities in social media are available to every business, from mom-and-pop shops to big Fortune 500s. Every company can make a positive impact on its audience and build relationships, but you have to make the commitment to understand your individual consumers and provide added value to their lives. Many new brands, even those owned by big companies, still start on social media with nothing. Those companies may be backed by more dollars and staff, but even a small start-up with a one-person social media marketing department can achieve similar or better results.

The strategies described in this book go beyond the simple idea of return on investment. We are talking about building a relationship with individuals in your audience, and the strategy you choose often melds with their interests. Each platform where you establish presence may employ a different strategy. How you implement these strategies depends on your goals and the metrics involved.

The Four Audience Metrics

Audience metrics on social media have four levels, the first of which is interest: Who has looked? This is generally the largest segment of your current target audience outside of those who are not aware. This includes anyone who has seen your content online but does not yet follow you and those who follow you and have only some exposure to your social accounts.

From there, interest graduates to engagement: Who has spoken? These are much smaller segments, generally 10% to 15% of the interested folks. This does not mean 85% of your audience is uninvolved. They are just passive, watching and waiting for an opportunity to participate when it makes sense to them.

The next level up is virality: Who has shared? This segment is slightly smaller, about 2% to 5% of your total audience. These people are very important, however, as they are the ones spreading your message to others who have yet to discover you. Keep in mind, not all the people who have shared your content are advocates. "Advocacy" can be defined in a number of ways. Generally speaking, if you have someone in your audience who is sharing your content regularly, praising your brand, or answering questions for other consumers, then they may be an advocate.

The final metric is purchase: Who is buying? How quickly a person graduates to buying depends on his or her needs, but, generally speaking, customers have gone through all four levels of interest by the time they make a purchase. They have seen your content, may have asked a question, made a comment, or engaged with your content in some way. They may also have shared your content, online, offline or immediately after purchase.

Achieving sales through social media is a journey. More often than not, it is a long journey that dwells in the intangible metrics of emotion — how you make your audience feel with your content — but eventually you give consumers reason to continue to follow your brand and they become a customer.

If you continue to engage the people who purchase and build relationships after the first sale, you can also create advocacy, which in turn generates more customers and grows your audience. The sooner you realize that long-term relationships built through social media will return more sales than you had dreamed of, the sooner you can get to work. Your return on investing in social media goes beyond clicks, conversion rates and currency. It begins with a goal of understanding your individual consumers and ultimately allows you to create an experience in which your audience wants to partake, one they are truly excited about.

There is a saying: "A friend will help you move; a true friend will help you move dead bodies." That is the difference in loyalty you can gain from a strong social media presence, so keep that in mind when considering adopting a presence on social media and establishing a community or relationship with your consumers. The people you build relationships with will forgive your faults, promote your successes, and defend you against naysayers. They are the people who will be there when you need them and they will be there for each other within the community — just like true friends.

The Branding Strategy

Your brand bell rings a special tone. Little nuances set it apart from a noisy world. Your audience relates to your voice, your tone and stance on specific topics. They may not always agree with your brand, but your audience will look beyond the small things with which they do not agree. They will trust a brand that portrays emotion and tries to connect with people, rather than behaving robotically. Much like they do with their friends, they embrace the parts of your brand they like and continue to support your brand. The Branding Strategy works with your audience's emotions more than any other strategy. Under this strategy, you want your audience to visit your channel for the emotions your brand evokes within them.

The Branding Strategy

A successful Branding Strategy begins with a great understanding of your brand. It requires your brand to have a stance on global issues and a distinct way of reacting to your competition and supplemental brands. More importantly, you should have guidelines and a standard for how you talk about topics that match your brand's tone.

One of the most notable examples of good reactions to supplemental brands is the exchange between Taco Bell and Old Spice on Twitter. Old Spice, being facetious, asked about Taco Bell's ingredients, and Taco Bell came back with a witty rebuttal. The exchange went like this:

> @OldSpice: Why is it that "fire sauce" isn't made with any real fire? Seems like false advertising.
> @TacoBell: @OldSpice Is your deodorant made with really old spices?
> @OldSpice: @TacoBell Depends. Do you consider volcanos, tanks and freedom to be spices?

Old Spice truly channeled its brand voice and Taco Bell stood its ground behind its product. When answering questions about your brand, be prepared to answer in your official voice, tone and style.

When Google+ launched in late 2011, there was a lot of fanfare about it marking the end of Twitter and Facebook. Though users generated a lot of mean-spirited content about other brands at the launch of G+, Google never repurposed that content because it didn't fit with its personality. Surely Google employees reveled in the rain of banter promoting the takeover by their new platform, but they never adopted the tone or spread the rumor. They clearly made an effort to present their developments in a civilized and professional manner. Google has always been known to talk "Google," and it thrives on innovation and creativity, much like its rotation of creative depictions of its logo on the homepage. The company has a light-hearted, nerdy sense of humor, but never talks down to competitors. Even its recent television spots for the Chrome browser only point out the benefits of the product, without any mention of competitors. It helps create a positive image.

As your audience grows, you will deal with a number of points of view and opinions of what's happening in the world, and you need to know where you stand and what actions you will take. You want to be in control of your content when using the Branding Strategy. Your brand is a sensitive creature and the public's opinion can be easily be swayed when not carefully managed. Under this strategy, you need to vet all content you post on your social media channels and protect it from outside influences. You cannot control what is posted in channels outside of your profiles, but you can control your channels and the voice you use daily.

The Branding Strategy

Failure to Lock Down

The biggest influences online are often the ones that also garner the worst commentary. It is just natural human instinct to either absolutely love or absolutely loathe something. This is why mediocrity does not get your brand anywhere in the online world. You have to be spectacularly great or spectacularly awful. Unfortunately, if your brand was not meant to represent the worst in the world, it can be damaging when your brand becomes the center of negative attention.

> *"It's Friday, Friday. Gotta get down on Friday. Everybody's lookin' forward to the weekend, weekend."*

Remember this song? Rebecca Black debuted her single online in March 2011. She became an overnight success in her failure. Her video blazed through the social networks, shared on every platform imaginable — often with the attached message: "OMG this is awful!"

Poor Rebecca Black just wanted to be a popular and well-liked pop artist. Unfortunately, the Internet took hold and ruined that dream. It began with a tweet from Michael J. Nelson, a comedian, who called her video "the worst video ever made." That is when Rebecca's infamy began, successfully gaining 167 million views and 3.6 million votes on YouTube — 3.1 million

You Get What You Give

of which were "dislikes." Only 14 days after its release, it surpassed the previously most disliked video, "Baby" by Justin Bieber.[1]

It had been publicly accepted that "Friday" was not going to become a hit when pop culture critics jumped on board. Lyndsey Parker from Yahoo! Music stated it could be "the worst song ever."[2] Kevin Rutherford from Billboard Magazine described it as something that could only be seen in its entirety to fully appreciate how awful it was.

The real issue is that, despite the dislikes, the video was getting a massive amount of commentary to support the growing laughter on the internet. By June 2011, only three months after its debut, the video was removed from YouTube[3] — a little too late to stop the negativity, to be honest. Even with an appearance in pop star Katy Perry's video "Friday Night," Rebecca Black's brand had been tarnished. She released her second single, "My Moment," on YouTube in November 2011. It didn't get nearly as much as attention — her 15 minutes had passed — and still had a majority vote of "dislike," with 590,000 dislikes to 340,000 likes by the end of the year.

The only hope for the Rebecca Black brand to come back would be if her manager and producers embraced her reputation as a joke. She is in a great position for parodies and cheesy slapstick appearances until a sliver of a moment where she may be able to redeem herself and be taken seriously by the public.

The Branding Strategy

The mistake in Black's campaign is that she and her parents didn't recognize the slippery slope of negativity and they did not act fast enough. As soon as it was apparent that the video was taking a turn for the worst (in late March before it passed Bieber's song as the most-disliked video on YouTube) the situation should have been locked down, the video removed and revamped. It was her only song; she didn't have anything to lose by taking it down. Had she removed it sooner, she may have had everything to gain with a popular comeback. With the understanding that Black had budgetary constraints — as any start-up would — the risks were high.

In contrast to the infamous failure of Rebecca Black, we must take look at 2012 YouTube sensation Psy and his 10-day record-breaker "Gangnam Style." Despite the lyrics being in Korean and the song coming from an artist who has been in the business for 12 years in Korea, the song took off in the United States and the rest of the world in a matter of days after being posted to YouTube in June 2012. Granted, there may have also been a big PR push that helped drive its success, but it also had other factors that helped it break through the noise and become successful through social media.

The video and song were already a parody, and parodies are already more likely to be shared repeatedly online and are more difficult to ridicule. The music style was also current and trending in the larger markets of the world, so the new audience was primed to like the song. Psy had also worked for an entire month to carefully choreograph his dance moves in the video. In an interview, Psy reports there was a lot of pressure on him to come out with something new.[4] The dance Psy does in the video is 100% manufactured. The new moves were designed to get people to emulate Psy's dancing. These new dance moves were the kindling for parody versions of the video to be produced and spread around the Internet via social media. The last factor that made "Gangnam Style" a sensation was celebrity tweets, just like the tweets that had set Rebecca Black's viral train wreck in motion. Celebrities like Katy Perry, Britney Spears, Ryan Seacrest and T-Pain — all music industry people — tweeted and shared the video with their audiences. Nelly Furtado also performed the song at her concert in the Philippines on August 16, only 2 months after its debut.

By September, Psy was featured on a number of television shows including *Saturday Night Live, Ellen, The Today Show* and *VH1 Morning Buzz Live*, which perpetuated the viral nature of the video. By embracing the parodies of the video and putting Psy front and center on mass media outlets with the carefully designed dance, "Gangnam Style" was branded for success. In just under six months after its release, the video had more than 1 billion views on YouTube, making it the first YouTube video to ever reach that milestone (shattering Black's record). The song was the No. 1 downloaded song on iTunes in 31 countries by the end of September 2012, with 2.7 million downloads, earning Psy $2.4 million.[5]

When it comes to your brand, no matter the risk, you want the public to hold it to the same light that you do. That means, less the threat of certain bankruptcy, your brand should be protected. As soon as Internet trolls and haters get their teeth into your mistakes, they will tear you apart. Your job is to make sure that doesn't happen.

Business Decisions and Racism

Lowe's was at the brink of disaster when it came to trolls on Facebook in early December 2011. The home improvement retailer had announced on its Facebook page that it would be pulling its ads from the TLC television show "*All-American Muslim.*" They announced this decision via a Facebook note, which garnered more than 23,000 comments in only a few days. Many of the posts were back-and-forth banter between pro- and anti-Muslim Lowe's Facebook fans. Lowe's had essentially created a forum for a discussion that was way off-brand.

The company was at risk of losing support for its brand. Aside from the direct commentary, thousands of users online were vowing to boycott any retailer embracing those values. The post even made it to the *Daily Show with Jon Stewart*. Many consumers questioned the intent behind the business decision to pull the advertising.

So where did Lowe's go wrong? For one, they posted a notice on Facebook! That decision did not need to be shared in the social media world. That was a business decision and certainly a tough one. It should have been posted on the company's official website, under the news section. If people on the Internet had decided to pick it up and discuss it, then, and only then, should the brand have felt it was required to address such a tough issue through its social media channels. Secondly, as soon as racist remarks were posted, someone on the Lowe's social media team should have deleted them and reminded the community about the posting guidelines for posting on the Lowe's Facebook page.

Better late than never, Lowe's did put out a response on Facebook explaining its stance on the comments and some insight to its reasoning. The company recognized its mistake, and in the response, which is no longer available, Lowe's also stated that it did not feel Facebook was an appropriate place to have that conversation. Since the incident, Lowe's has done well and reported no lasting effect on its sales.

But of course, in some cases, trolls are inevitable. People are entitled to their opinions, but that doesn't mean it should taint your brand. If you're legitimately concerned about trolls, there are some measures you can take. Avoid releasing content that blatantly invites hazing. If you find your brand in the midst of a troll attack and have no way of reconciling the situation, lock down the content causing the stir. You are better off removing the content that is causing the serious backlash, than waiting out the storm.

Placing Your Brand

Multiple successful implementations of the Branding Strategy can be found with Coca-Cola. The sheer depth of the company's history is a prime example of the ebb and flow of a brand's challenges and the evolution of branding with new technologies. Coke is, to this day, one of the healthiest brands on social media, with more than 70 million Facebook likes, 150 million views on thousands of videos on YouTube and nearly 2 million Twitter followers.

What is astonishing about Coca-Cola is its ability to put the right branding in the right places. The company keeps its branding in a fairly closed loop and maintains great integrity with its audience. On Facebook, it only shares its posts on the wall to keep it clean and only the Coca-Cola "voice" is seen by page visitors; consumer-generated content is kept under the "posts by others" section. Coke never shares its audience's content on Facebook. On YouTube, it puts out specialized content that relates well to the community; not just commercials, but heartfelt stories about how the brand has brought people together, which supports its long-term campaign of spreading happiness. On a blog post titled "Coke Conversation," the company embraces Coke lovers from the past by sharing the history of its brand and showing off retro swag.

In 2011, Coca-Cola jumped onto Tumblr. This was a shrewd move because of Tumblr's favorable demographics, as Tumblr has taken off with teens and young adults. Coke is now putting its brand in front of its future audience and embracing them with content that they enjoy. On Tumblr, Coke will grow up with the audience and share content that's relevant to them into the future. It is quite honestly what every cigarette company wishes it could do.

But Coca-Cola isn't the only company with a presence on Tumblr. In its midst are Whole Foods, Target, Vans and Sephora. And those are only the tip of the iceberg. There are more than 50 big brands using Tumblr, and some of them are doing it quite well.

That kind of market-anticipating move is what you can expect from Coke on all its platforms. It has constantly put out content that fits the audience of the platform on which it is posting. It understands its brand and has a clear vision for the future. When it comes to branding, Coca-Cola embraces the positive influence of its audience by giving them a way to share their content on a number of networks.

Companies on a smaller budget can be just as effective. Content is fairly cheap to produce and, if necessary, license-free images can be used. Learning about your audience, how they talk and why they love your brand requires time and due diligence. Armed with that knowledge and aimed in the correct direction, effective content can be executed by a company of any size.

The Branding Strategy is rooted in matching the values of your audience with that of your brand. Support their values and remind your audience that you share a similar outlook. Make them feel good and your audience will reciprocate by making your brand better. The customer now has much more control of brands than ever before. A single person has the ability to reach thousands of peers with a single post and can push their opinions out into the world where they will likely stay forever. It is imperative that brands keep their audiences happy to keep the brand in good standing. A strong relationship with your audience ensures that your faults are forgotten and your good actions are celebrated.

You Get What You Give

Endnotes

1 Matyszczyk, Chris. CNET, "Rebecca Black passes Bieber as YouTube's most hated video." March 29, 2011. http://news.cnet.com/8301-17852_3-20048534-71.html.

2 Parker, Lyndsey. Yahoo!Music, "Is YouTube Sensation Rebecca Black's "Friday" The Worst Song Ever?." March 13, 2011. http://music.yahoo.com/blogs/stop-the-presses/is-youtube-sensation-rebecca-blacks-friday-the-worst-song-ever.html.

3 Swash, Rosie. The Guardian, "Rebecca Black's Friday video removed from YouTube." June 17, 2011. http://www.theguardian.com/music/2011/jun/17/rebecca-black-friday-video-youtube.

4 Ryzik, Melena. The New York Times, "His Style Is Gangnam, and Viral Too." Oct. 11, 2012. http://www.nytimes.com/2012/10/14/arts/music/interview-psy-the-artist-behind-gangnam-style.html?_r=1&.

5 Warner, Brian. Celebrity Net Worth, "Psy Net Worth." http://www.celebritynetworth.com/richest-celebrities/richest-rappers/psy-net-worth.

The Customer Service Strategy

Your customers have always had a voice; you just were not always able to listen. Social media tools have given you a proverbial window to watch and listen in on conversations people are publicly having around your brand. When social media is used correctly, you can fix the issues they encounter and also change the minds of unhappy consumers who might otherwise have fled to your competition.

For every customer complaint, there are 26 other silent and unhappy customers who have not spoken up. A customer is four times more likely to go to a competing company if the problem was service-related, rather than related to price or product.[1] Social media customer service representatives stand to have a huge impact on your business through customer retention alone.

The Customer Service strategy requires a timely response and, as the Internet continues to accelerate at the speed at which information travels, you are going to need to get as close to real-time as possible in both listening and responding. I purposefully chose the phrase "timely response" rather than "quick response" for a number of reasons. For one, "timely" implies a favorable time span, one that is understood by both parties as reasonable. Some issues will take time and research to solve and literally cannot be done quickly. Secondly, "quick" implies that you rush. You do not need to rush! Rushing opens the opportunity for mistakes and cursory answers.

It is best to serve your customers completely and clearly. This strategy also requires a complete openness and acceptance of your failures. You are giving your audience a place to speak its mind, and you should respect all the resulting opinions. In return, you will get the respect of your audience. Admitting to your shortcomings when they occur builds trust with your customers and shows that you are not a brand that tries to put a favorable spin on an obvious mistake. You have to mean it when you apologize and cannot use an apology as an excuse to make mistakes regularly!

The Customer Service Strategy

The customer service strategy boils down to one basic concept: KISS — Keep It Simple, Stupid. The goal of customer service is to solve problems as directly and in as timely a manner as possible. The same goes for customer service online. The Customer Service Strategy is the toughest strategy to implement effectively because you will have a tendency to use traditional tactics to serve your consumer, but it's traditional tactics that lead so many people to social media for answers in the first place. They weren't getting the answer they wanted through traditional forums, so they started shouting in a place where everyone could hear them.

In many ways, social media changed the way companies thought about customer service. It allowed them to open a channel to listen to customer complaints that were not heard in the past. A lot of the software developed around social media listening has incorporated sentiment analysis as well. You can now hear what they are saying, and also gain a general consensus of the mood and tone of the groups of people talking about your brand. Granted, sentiment analysis is currently only 60% accurate, and may require additional manual adjustment, but it is more information than was previously available.

The open channels that social media provides are a two-way street. By participating in Twitter, Facebook and commenting on blogs, brands can service their customers in near real-time. While customers may tweet, blog and post about their experiences, brands can also leave answers to frequently asked questions in the places their audience is most likely to discover them. In addition to the brand website, brands or their employees can participate in the conversations on their customers' websites as well. These channels are static and the content placed there can show up in online search, where other customers may be looking.

However, what many companies, especially those in service industries, found was that there was an overwhelming amount of people already talking about their brands online and many of these comments were dispersed across the Internet. There were so many comments to answer on blogs, Facebook posts and tweets that it seemed unmanageable. The solution to this problem is to invest in a centralized channel for all those questions to openly be asked and to create a forum for needs to be expressed. Setting your camp in one place where your audience can go to share their comments directly with you helps you manage the volume more effectively. By centralizing the content, this channel is also more easily discovered by consumers using search to look for answers. It is still, however, recommended that companies participate in some of the larger dispersed channels in addition to a central channel.

As connected as consumers are today, and with the increasing connectivity that mobile technology allows, many customers are going online first to find the answers they seek.

They are relying more and more on search, their personal networks and social media platforms to get the answers to a problem with minimal effort. It is no wonder that many marketers are planning to double their spending on social media in the next five years.[2] All these companies want to be on the forefront of their customers' inquiries. More are joining this trend, but many still have an insufficient process for handling their customers online.

With social media and a decent listening campaign, you can be prompt when answering consumer questions on public channels. However, you must have some forethought. Listen to what questions are being asked most often and have a policy and guide for your social media team to answer questions in a timely manner. Answering questions is only one of the tactics for this strategy. To make your strategy a success, you must connect these tactics to a business goal, such as decreased churn or increased net promoter score to truly measure the effect of your Customer Service Strategy.

The Power of 'Sorry'

When it comes to customer service, it goes against instinct for a company to own up to its faults. Shining a light on the things a company does wrong seems to go against the whole concept of seeking profits. When a company makes mistakes and makes money in the process, leaving customers unfulfilled but still taking their money, it seems like a scam. From a company perspective, unless the business is in serious trouble, complaints only occur once every couple thousand transactions. But consider a complaint from the perspective of the customer, and you have a much different story.

Tom Farmer and Shane Atchison have such a story. They published "Yours Is A Very Bad Hotel," a PowerPoint presentation about their bad experience at a Double Tree Hotel, which they put online. It only took one night clerk at one hotel for these two men to write off the Double Tree Hotel chain entirely.

Farmer and Atchison were unable to get the room they had reserved because the hotel was in the practice of overbooking, which is when a hotel books more rooms than it has capacity for, with the expectation that a certain percentage of guests will not show up to claim their reservations. Farmer and Atchison were international travelers and likely had never stayed at this particular hotel or the chain before and were "walked" — a term used in the industry to turn away people who fit these criteria. Aside from not getting a room, the two men were most upset by the way the night clerk, Mike, was unapologetic, unsympathetic and unwilling to find them accommodations elsewhere. In response, the travelers put together their PowerPoint

The Customer Service Strategy

presentation based on the bad service they had received. The presentation even included snarky statistics comparing the likelihood of Earth being ejected from the solar system by the gravitational pull of a passing star — 1: 2,200,000 — and the odds of their booking a room at the Double Tree again — "worse than that."[3] The presentation earned Farmer and Atchison quite a bit of good publicity, while the Double Tree brand only garnered negative publicity.

From Mike the night clerk's perspective, these two men were only two out of hundreds that he had served that night – a small percentage. Moreover, the hotel was full, so the hotel was making the bottom line and, as far as Mike was concerned, that was enough. From Farmer and Atchison's perspective, they were greatly mistreated and literally thrown into the street in the middle of the night despite having reservations at the hotel. Granted, that hotel could not take them in, but with some sympathy and sense of service, the hotel could have helped them find rooms at nearby competitors, a move that would have gone a long way toward appeasing them, and would have cost all but a few minutes of Mike's time. Most importantly, Mike could have apologized.

Apologies go a very long way; farther than you might think. A study by behavioral economist Dan Ariely found that an apology has amazing power — so much power that it could have persuaded Farmer and Atchison from ever creating the PR blitz PowerPoint.

For Ariely's study, a young man was hired to run a simple test in a coffee shop. In this test, the man would walk up to a person sitting alone and offer them five dollars to participate in a five-minute test. The test was a menial task of finding adjacent pairs of letters in a grid of letters. After five minutes, the man would come back, give the participant a receipt and cash, asking them to count the money and sign the receipt as confirmation they had received the five dollars. This was the control group. There were two other test groups. One group went through the same scenario, but in the middle of explaining the task, the man pretended to take a fake, 12-second phone call, then proceeded to explain the task without addressing that the call ever occurred. This was the annoyance group, as taking a call during the explanation is considered rude. The last group was the apology group, where, just like in the annoyance group, the man took a call, and then proceeded to explain the task. The difference in the apology group came when he dropped off the receipt and money. When handing over the payment, the man would pause and apologize for taking the call, saying, "I'm sorry, I should not have taken that call. That was rude of me."

So how did Ariely measure the impact of an apology? When the man was giving the cash and receipt to the recipient, he always overpaid the subject, leaving two to four dollars more than expected. The hypothesis was that the people in the control group, who had no phone call during the explanation, would not take or "steal" the extra money that was given to them. Shockingly, only 46% of the control group returned the extra cash. In the annoyance group, a mere 14% of the people who were interrupted with a phone call returned the extra cash. However, most astonishing were the results from the apology group. With an apology, the effect of the annoyance was completely erased, with 46% of the apology group returning the money, just like the control group.[4]

This effect has been measured in a number of ways, and the results all support each other. An apology means so much more to a person than compensation. Having a bit of human empathy can erase the vengeful feelings an upset customer might have, even if it comes from a brand. Whether it is the customer service care team on the phone, or the customer service team on social media behind the brand, recognition of the issue and an earnest apology to the customer for the discomfort caused by that issue makes the customer feel more at ease. In situations like these, having a human voice for the brand and acting with real human feeling will make the biggest impact. The cases where a service team member will need to go above and beyond are few and far between, especially if the company is in good standing. But an apology, in any case, will go a long way.

You Get What You Give

Travel and the Customer Service Strategy

Despite their training for employees, the hospitality and travel industry is not "getting it" when it comes to serving customers online. You would think that for an industry based around customer service, it would lead the pack, but unfortunately many do not. The trouble is that these companies are relying heavily on traditional methods to answer consumers' issues and have so far failed to pick up the pace and get answers in front of the consumer.

Choice Hotels was late to jump in to the social media game and also did not think very far ahead. By the end of 2012, the company had fewer than 1,500 tweets with its verified Twitter account (@ChoiceHotels), and it had barely gotten started with Facebook. This company has an amazing opportunity to connect with its consumers and to service them through channels where customers already participate and are talking about the company.

Each of the Choice Hotels' 11 brands has an average of 10 mentions on Twitter a day — some complaints, some praise. In 2011, the only outgoing messages from Choice's Twitter account were in response to complaints. Here is what they said:

> "Please contact us regarding your recent experience at chtwitter@choicehotels.com. We would like the opportunity to assist."

That is not an answer to a concern. It is a brush-off. This kind of response causes a consumer to seek an answer somewhere else. Consumers are not stupid. They can find an email address on a website. They go to real-time, conversational channels because they want to talk to someone. Here is what a consumer reads when they receive that kind of response:

"We don't really care, but if you're mad enough, try us at our email address so we can get back to you at our convenience."

In 2012, Choice moved away from that tactic and now does not answer complaints. The brand simply pushes out promotional content on its channel. It does not display any information in the Twitter bio about how to get customer service. It is not surprising that this brand has less than 1,500 tweets. It's a grossly underused opportunity for service on its part, especially considering consumers are there and looking for help.

Its Facebook presence is much better, despite its customers' remodeling to use it as a customer service platform. It was initially set up as a promotional presence. Choice does answer some complaints, but it chooses which it will respond to on the platform. Its choice of who to serve is not random — there certainly must be some prioritization method, but it does not treat each customer the same. These Facebook responses also

You Get What You Give

include requests to email the Choice team. The brand also does not respond to all the praise.

Keep in mind when implementing the Customer Service Strategy that you must not alienate individuals, especially those that praise you. Some complainers just want recognition. Leaving questions and praise unanswered makes the brand seem uninterested in helping and being part of the solution. Even if some of these issues are addressed offline, other people in the audience only see an unresponsive brand. Choice could make a better effort of using either Twitter or Facebook as its customer service channel and leave instructions on the other on how to reach its online service team.

Choice Hotels is not the only brand with these issues. Travelocity makes the same mistake. Travelocity does a better job of handling praise and the community, but still answers customer service issues with a request to email. These responses are neither timely nor direct. They push consumers into a queue, making them wait in line to stew in their anger. Consumers now are expecting faster response times online. They want to know someone is looking into their questions in seconds, not minutes, and certainly not at the cost of any extra effort. They do not necessarily expect the answer right away, just an assurance that their issues are being handled.

JetBlue has it right. This company implemented the "Bill of Rights," which answers most of the frequently asked questions,

The Customer Service Strategy

and all others are sent to its hotline. If you search for JetBlue on Twitter, you will see a link to the Bill of Rights in the company's bio. If someone with a complaint posts on Facebook, JetBlue refers him or her to the Bill of Rights with a link.

Your company can go a step further. If you truly want to solve your consumers' issues, have a place they can go to discover the answer themselves. This hub should include your answers as a brand, and should consolidate your other customers' answers and empower them to answer each other's inquires if they wish. It should be easy to navigate. It should be mobile-responsive and formatted for a variety of devices. (There are a number of services that can help you achieve this.) The hub should also give users a secondary option, clearly posted and apparent.

That second option is up to you. It could be a hotline, text message line, live chat, or an email address. Whatever you choose, it should give the feeling of gratification and it should be immediate. An email should be answered immediately, whether automatically or manually sent by a person, with a message that assures the consumer that his or her issue is being addressed. Include an estimated time of response; that response time should be met or exceeded. If there is a delay in finding a solution, the situation should be communicated to the individual. Send an email explaining what is happening. A little handholding takes a few moments of your time, but stops the clock for your customers. They won't feel like they have been waiting as long and now know what is happening behind the curtain. Communication that sets expectations relieves the mystery and frustration that comes with customer service.

The best option is to have a live person on that channel to give customers the answers they are looking for. This is where your social media policy and guide to customer service for your team comes into play. Your social media team should be empowered to find the answers and provide them online, immediately. If you choose your platform for the customer service strategy to be a forum, Twitter, or Facebook, the team should be available at a second's notice.

Your customer service channel does not have to be active for 24 hours. Feel free to put hours of operation around this strategy. But make it clear, reasonable, and build your consumers' expectations. Often consumers just want to know that something is happening or when your service team will give attention to their requests.

Depending on your industry, you may handle personal customer information. When it comes to sensitive information such addresses, emails, or card or member numbers, you should have a protocol to move the conversation into a private medium. Facebook and Twitter both offer options to communicate with individuals on a one-on-one basis that is not publicly viewable.

These more immediate options should be used before a request to email.

Tech and Response

Cox Communications runs its Facebook like a customer service counter. Consumers go to the page and frequently post questions about outages, billing and, sometimes, serious customer service neglect. These customers are met by a person with a pleasing tone and helpful intent, just as they would if they were approaching a customer service representative in any department store.

Complaints about past customer service issues that have reference numbers are escalated immediately to a Cox Communications representative, and these responses are more personal and ask for specific information. Customers rarely receive a scripted response, which gives the impression that work is being done on the back-end. Responses are often received within 30 minutes of the customer's post. They look like this:

> *"Yikes Dan! I truly apologize that you have had this type of experience. I can understand why you would be upset, I would be also. I want to look into this further. Please email me your street address to coxhelp@cox.com. Thanks, Tiff"*

You Get What You Give

A real human being answers the consumer's call. That is the epitome of good online customer service.

Questions about outages in service are answered with legitimate reasons. Compensation is often offered for the inconvenience. Billing questions are often answered by references to a standard bill layout so that consumers can locate information on their own. The Cox Communications social media team helps people find the answers with the materials the consumer has at hand.

> "Linda, your feedback has been submitted to our programming team. Please continue to keep an eye on the News From Cox section of your bill, where we announce channel additions, new services, etc. –Renee"

> "Hi Jane, what area are you currently located in? I can ensure that your feedback is heard. –Renee"

Best of all, these questions are answered publicly. This works in Cox's favor for two reasons. One, it shows the company's commitment to open communication. It's not afraid of the complaints, which builds a sense of confidence that it can answer all consumer questions. It doesn't hide complaining posts, but rather leaves them up for all to see. Two, the fact that others can see these complaints means that people with the same questions can follow along and discover the answers they need

The Customer Service Strategy

or follow suit and contact, via email, the representative on duty for that time. This all leads to happy and satisfied customers.

Best Buy's Geek Squad also runs its Facebook page in a similar manner. Technical questions are answered by a knowledgeable squad member. The company even answers specific questions about hardware and software issues, which shows it stays true to its geeky brand. Responses are timely, direct, and give complete answers to questions. Consumers do not need to go anywhere else to find their solutions, which is the key to the Customer Service Strategy. Consumers' tolerance for the "run around" is at an all-time low.

Fashion Statements

When it comes to customer service success while maintaining a great brand voice, look no further than the men's fashion brand Bonobos. The company has a pun-inspired voice with weekly emails that will make you smile and a team of customer service "Ninjas" to help you choose your next garb. Its single promise is that it sells better-fitting clothes, and, as any online shopper can tell you, finding clothes that fit without trying them on can be a challenge.

Bonobos solves the fitting room dilemma with its Twitter "Ninjas" and a fit guide. The guide is easily accessible on the website next to any item you plan on purchasing. If you have a concern about the size or fit of an item, shoot a tweet to @BonobosNinjas and, in a matter of minutes, not hours, you will have an answer. Or, if you are feeling especially testy, try not mentioning them directly and just using the Bonobos name. The Ninjas will seek you out and still give you the answer you need.

The company does an excellent job managing customer expectations and making suggestions on matching items. The Ninjas treat every customer as an individual and offer all solutions for that customer alone, rather than bucketing people into generalized groups. The service team is also very informed on all the items listed on the website and provide a lot of value when questions about purchases occur.

The Ninjas do not stop at Twitter; you can expect surprisingly quick replies on Facebook as well. So fast, in fact, you might check behind you to see if they were reading over your shoulder as you were typing. All answers are custom-tailored for the inquirer and give full answers with no run-around. All questions are answered and the majority of praise receives a comment as well.

The pun humor engrained in the brand is used tactfully and carefully in the customer service arena. Bonobos has a strong understanding of its voice, but uses it carefully and does not let it interfere with the customer service process. Humor is rarely used when answering a consumer question, no matter how seriously it is asked; however, it may slip in a pun every now and again.

Overall, Bonobos spends more time answering and responding to customer questions and driving individual conversation with its audience members than it does promoting its own content. The brand definitely gives a lot to its customers and it gets it back in spades. Even if customers are not asking Bonobos a question directly, the team listens for audience tweets that use the brand name or product names, and reaches out to them. That is the epitome of the Customer Service Strategy, as each customer service ticket helps drive the brand and its promise of assistance in sales even when customers least expect it.

Endnotes

1 Shaw, Colin. Beyond Philosophy, " 15 Statistics That Should Change the Business World – But Haven't." June 10, 2013. http://www.beyondphilosophy.com/blog/15-statistics-that-should-change-the-business-world-but-havent.

2 Lester, Traci. ASPE ROI, "2013 CMO Survey Results." June 21, 2013. http://www.aspe-roi.com/blog/the-2013-cmo-survey-results/.

3 Atchison, Shane, and Tom Farmer. "Yours Is a Very Bad Hotel." March 30, 2007. http://www.slideshare.net/politicsjunkie/yours-is-a-very-bad-hotel.

4 Ariely, Dan. The Upside of Irrationality: The Unexpected Benefits of Defying Logic at Work and at Home. New York: HarperCollins, 2010.

The Community Experience Strategy

A community drives itself and, like a flock of birds, a clear leader is often indistinguishable. The Community Experience Strategy is a careful balance of interaction and brand management. It works much like a 16th-century court where you sit as the king and all your subjects reside beside you. These people are typically the most active in your audience. They may struggle with each other for your attention, they may take issue with you or your policies, but as a whole they represent the greater population. They each have their own agenda, but you

The Community Experience Strategy

are the law of the land and they must play by your rules. You must be one with the people, your entire court and the leaders of the land. There will be sour grapes and you will be held accountable for all the good and bad that happen in your kingdom. You can keep your people happy by letting them know they are being heard and that their interests are being taken into account, and by doing so your kingdom will thrive! That is what "you get what you give" is all about.

The Community Experience Strategy hinges on two intangible quantifiers of your social presence: the conversation between consumers about your brand, and your conversation with consumers. Some social media networks work well to keep your audience engaged with one another and their conversations easily searchable. How you want to structure your conversations and whether you want the historical conversation to be discoverable will determine which platform you choose. Twitter is a real-time stream of conversation and works well for large groups to have multiple simultaneous conversations. Facebook, on the other hand, has threaded comments that keep conversations in one place, and notifications of conversations go out to those users engaged only in those threads.

Your audience's feelings may also vary from day to day. The experience for any one individual can be difficult to gauge; however, listening to the overall sentiment of your audience as they talk with one another will tell you their current feelings toward your brand and topics being discussed amongst them. The challenge with the Community Experience Strategy is that public opinion has an ebb and flow depending on the circumstances surrounding your brand that particular week or day. This also means you will need to become educated in all things that influence your brand, as well as all things your brand influences. For instance, you may be a doctor, and New York City's attempt to ban large sodas might have influenced how people talk about your brand or industry. This is a time when your stances on social issues will come into play.

Generally when complaints occur in the community, they are about circumstances outside of your control. This could include anything from issues with your third-party distribution channel, weather, laws and even other customers. The key is to have a stance on common issues and problems. However, do not confuse the Community Experience Strategy for the Customer Service Strategy. Individuals in your audience may tempt you to answer concerns directly about your brand, service or products. These questions need to be directed to the proper channels. The focus of the Community Experience Strategy is not to solve problems and transact compensation, but rather to give your audience a place to talk about your brand and their experiences. You are there to engage in conversation and recognize the praise and love your audience has for your brand and entertain them with content that gives your audience more reasons to love it. If you must answer service questions, answer them privately to keep the momentum of your community.

Your channel for this strategy needs to enable your audience to share. Trends in social media indicate that richer content, such as photos and short videos, is better shared — just keep your posting guidelines in mind. One tactic you can use to gain leverage with your audience's own content is to repurpose theirs. This allows you to praise your audience and make them feel included by giving them credit for the highlighted content. This also shows that you are aware of and support their interests. Encourage your audience to post brand-related content and, with permission, repurpose and distribute their content to share with the rest of the community. The more inviting you make the community, the more your audience will share. Recognition and thanks will bring the individuals in your audience together. As a whole, they will have a group experience that nurtures an affinity for your brand.

With any community, you should establish traditions. Welcome newcomers to the arena daily or weekly and post holiday updates that unite everyone through individual participation. These activities give your brand an opportunity to engage your audience about their passions. For instance, a brand such as KitchenAid could benefit immensely from the Community Engagement Strategy. Amateur and professional bakers and pastry chefs alike view KitchenAid with the highest regard. KitchenAid could enrich its engagement by hosting a chat around cooking and baking and giving its community a place to share recipes, photos of food and food preparation. Giving customers who already love the brand a place to explore their passions can create a stronger, self-perpetuating, emotional connection to the brand. Alas, KitchenAid has yet to implement this strategy on any appropriate channel.

Make Them Feel Special

Your community is made up of people. Real people. As people, they have needs, which can be described by Maslow's hierarchy of needs: food, shelter, friends, esteem and recognition. You can be safe in the assumption that if they are buying your brand, you will not need to provide food or shelter, but you will need to give a sense of esteem and in some cases even fulfill the need for belonging. This is where using a conversational voice and behaving like a friend becomes very important and effective for your brand.

As your brand leads the community of fans and advocates, it must constantly remind them why they are there. In the "you get what you give" ecosystem, to gain more love, you must give more. Over time, your audience will become accustomed to your day-to-day content. Unless they are engaged creatively or have a reason to come back regularly, they will fade away over time. This is inevitable. As a brand on social media, part of your mission is to perpetuate the affinity for your brand by getting new people to join your audience and by creating stories that attract your fans' friends. "Likes" and praising comments can be effective and tactful, but you must also create actions that can support the business goals of your brand. You are a business and must run like a business, so it's understandable that entertaining your consumers and making them feel involved can be difficult to justify when you still need to make ends meet.

There is one tactic you can use to give your community members a feeling of belonging and still create opportunities that drive your business. It's a very basic concept, but highly effective. It's producing exclusive content. This tactic gives you leverage over the content you are already creating and allows you to make your community feel special. By giving your community access to content under the umbrella of "insider" knowledge, you give them a sense of belonging and attachment.

"Exclusive" does not mean that you simply slap a "top secret" stamp on it and then give it to everyone. Insiders must be granted access. There must be an exchange between the individuals who want your content and your brand. Your audience gives you something of value— their email addresses, for example — and in exchange for trusting you with their

You Get What You Give

information, you trust them with content that can only they can access.

"Trust" is the key word. Abuse that trust and you will devalue anything behind the door of exclusivity. Your community is made of smart individuals and they will not be drawn in by tomfoolery or false promises. If you abuse the trust and start spamming them or opt them into communications that are unwanted or do not add value to the experience, it just became clear your "exclusivity" is a guise for marketing. The information your audience exchanges with you should drive your business metrics. With some clever implementation, the exchange can even take on a game format.

A prime example of exclusive content that creates a special feeling is Conan O'Brien's F*Cards. With the simple act of "liking" the Team Coco Facebook page, an individual gains access to a series of videos featuring Conan that can be sent to his or her friends on Facebook. These videos are the perfect blend of the Conan brand and Facebook faux pas humor. These videos also go beyond just connecting with the community. This type of exclusive content works well because it empowers Conan fans to share their love for Conan while participating in the community through sharing the content with their friends. All the while, Conan is gaining permission to share new offers, show times and events with the new fans.

The Community Experience Strategy

Another great example is *The Daily Show*. True fans of Jon Stewart love his interview style, but the show is limited to about 23 minutes of airtime, so when Stewart gets a great guest, there is never enough time to show the whole interview. Unfortunately for Jon Stewart fans, some of the questions that may come under censorship restrictions or that run over the airtime are edited out. The solution for *The Daily Show* brand was to offer full interviews and extra content online to the community. On The Daily Show website, the online community can watch extra content and comment on the videos at their leisure. The interactions on the website also give the community a place to voice their opinions on the show's content — good and bad — which producers and writers can leverage for future show content. The exchange of comments creates better show content and hopefully grows viewership.

Jet Blue and Community

An interesting implementation of social media took place in 2006. This was back when Twitter was fairly new and many users were still under the impression that the more followers one had, the more you would benefit from the platform. However, @JetBlue began following users who mentioned them with the intention of listening for opportunities to help. In February 2007,

JetBlue initiated the aforementioned customer "Bill of Rights" in response to a delay on the tarmac that resulted in customer meltdowns. These two acts kick-started a new kind of brand loyalty with its audience.

JetBlue customers now have the knowledge that JetBlue is listening and that the company has a document that entitles customers to clearly outlined compensation when the promise of service is not kept. JetBlue got all the messy stuff out of the way so it could concentrate on the experience of travel and on talking with their audience about why they fly and where they are flying.

JetBlue's official Twitter bio reads:

> *"@JetBlue doesn't respond to formal complaints on Twitter. For official customer concerns, go to jetblue.com/speakup or call 1-800-jetblue."*

The company has made it clear that it will not answer customer service questions on Twitter, and it sticks to it! A few of the in-between posts are acknowledgements of complaints, but they are always escalated to the Bill of Rights. JetBlue allows its promise and Bill of Rights to help audience help itself, while its presence drives the community experience.

The majority of JetBlue's Twitter stream is dedicated to welcoming passengers boarding flights and passing along praise for its crew. Twitter is used as an immediate response to make travelers feel welcome and give them a sense that they are not alone on their travels. JetBlue is constantly listening and prepared to engage with its audience about their experiences while traveling or waiting in airport terminals.

Twitter is just the front line of the Community Experience Strategy with social media. What is more impressive is JetBlue's implementation of community on its Facebook page — it is a true hub of rich media generated by a national community. Travelers post pictures of JetBlue planes and the places they have traveled. JetBlue is right there alongside its community, sharing images and videos of its staff working and volunteering in the community and highlighting special guests on flights.

A significant game-changer for the company is that JetBlue has empowered employees, outside of the JetBlue community managers, to post comments and responses to posts by travelers. You can expect to see responses from employees like Joel Carmona, a curriculum developer for JetBlue University; Ethan Stein, an analyst for JetBlue; and Gregory G., who worked in Airport Operations. JetBlue embraced social media as a family and empowered its employees to be a part of the community alongside its audience.

A Lesson in Community

Consider all the members and micro-segments that make up your community. Each individual has his or her own voice and relates with your brand for his or her own reasons. When running your community, remember to embrace all of your individuals, give them equal voice and don't endorse or single out any one segment.

In September 2011, the traditional Italian pasta sauce maker Ragu made a big stain on the blogging tablecloth. The company's marketing team got ahead of itself and endorsed a turf war. Ragu put together a series of clips of mothers describing their experiences cooking with their kids, but it made the focus of the video comparing mommy's experiences with the way daddy did the cooking. The production of the clips made dads look dumb. If that jab wasn't bad enough, it purposefully called attention to the videos by tweeting links to key daddy bloggers during the campaign to ask them what they thought, and then falling silent. It was the social media equivalent to a sucker punch.

Arguably Ragu's primary audience is women. It makes sense that the company wanted to endorse its biggest fans, but in this case it pitted the majority against the minority with its videos. Although the brand wanted to encourage dads to participate

The Community Experience Strategy

more with the brand, a few of these videos came off as just plain mean.

Daddy bloggers were outraged! "Ragu hates Dads," by C.C. Chapman, kicked off the movement in social media. Chapman is the founder of Cast of Dads (castofdads.com), a podcast with four other fathers that covers topics regarding fatherhood, and Digital Dads (digitaldads.com), a website for dads where "a dad can be a guy." Chapman was a recipient of one of Ragu's tweets and was upset that Ragu had suggested that dads could not cook.[1] He took his experience and turned to his community to make a stand. Chapman's posts and tweets were well-received, and many supported the cause. Even some moms joined the fight to defend their counterparts. For Ragu, it was a social media nightmare.

The word-of-mouth message created by Chapman surrounding Ragu's campaign was backlash. Rather than successfully touching its target audience and strengthening advocacy of the brand through video, Ragu created a ripple that tore through its community. More was lost than was gained, all because the company did not follow the golden rule of community: Alienate no one. In the beginning, Ragu did not respond to the backlash. After a second blog post by Chapman, Ragu and two agency representatives reached out to him to discuss the campaign. He gave them his point of view and Ragu admitted its goal was not to alienate dads, but rather to engage them. Obviously, mistakes were made.

The unfortunate part of the campaign is that it could have easily been avoided. A small tweak in messaging to focus on dads' positive experiences of cooking with their kids rather than comparing them negatively to mothers would have strengthened the brand relationship with dads without any alienation. An even better campaign would have been a fair opportunity for moms and dads to talk about their experiences individually and why they enjoy the brand and cooking with kids. Mom and dads with equal voices, comparing their positive experiences, would have made for better content. This could have been a playful turf war and a fair opportunity for both sides to play a part in the story. The approach could have even extended into different ideas and contests. Ragu has since recovered from the campaign, but had to rebuild trust with their community. Some of those bloggers will never forget — and rightfully so.

Empowering Employees

IBM is one of the largest companies taking on social and doing it right — especially in the business-to-business world. As early as 1997, Big Blue took steps that led it to become what it calls a "social business." It formulated the social guidelines and

The Community Experience Strategy

practices in a unique way and even trained 3,000 of its employees to become content creators. IBM recognized that all companies were becoming media companies by creating content to add to conversations being had by consumers online, and so they pursued the creation of a platform that their employees could use to add to those conversations.

IBM was bold enough to allow employees to guide its social media policy and guidelines, using a wiki to formulate the document. It also regularly educates employees on topics such as social media best practices to help its team be the best it can be online. All this effort to train employees has had a great payoff. It has helped IBM become one of the most participatory Fortune 100 companies on social media. Ethan McCarty, director of social strategy and programs at IBM, is quoted in a Fast Company article as saying, "Good conversation creates good outcomes and that brings value to the organization and to the individual."[2]

The key to IBM's success on social media is its distinct definition of channels versus networks. The company as a whole does not confuse marketing channels with online networks, at risk of creating "spammy" messages. The company also has protocols and standards for creating content such as video, images and infographics, which are all driven by a firm grasp of its brand and guidelines. Most importantly, IBM believes that part of becoming a social business is that the company's employees are front and center of all digital activities. Many of the IBMers blog for the company, while some write their own blogs and others tweet or participate on LinkedIn.

IBM created the "Voices" platform, a public iteration of an intranet where employees could collaborate and chat. It grew to have custom feeds and feedback options that drove discussion. Now it lives as the hub for content distribution from IBMers across the Web. The best content from all those who participate in IBM's social activities through blogs, Twitter, and rich media is found on the specially designed Voices site.

On LinkedIn, IBM has created a community of more than 1 million users. The company views LinkedIn not only as a great marketing platform, but also as a place for employees to engage with consumers. As LinkedIn is more professional in nature, IBM encourages employees to participate in a professional manner. "Usage of the site is trending a lot more toward professional content consumption — it's not videos of cats," said McCarty.[3]

IBM understands the fundamentals of social media. As a B2B company, it faces the challenge of being interesting to the consumer as a person. By empowering its employees to participate, driving their interaction through training, and recognizing and understanding that content must add value and not just drive interactions, the company has become a screaming success on social media.

Seasons For Success

One hospitality and hotel brand that is getting social media right is Four Seasons. Perhaps it's the dedication to the principles of a concierge, or maybe the company is truly listening to its customers; either way, Four Seasons is taking social to the next level. It has set out to fulfill its audience's needs through online content. The company has realized there is much more to taking a trip that just booking the hotel. There are the places to see, shop, eat and be entertained, and all of these are taken into account through the content it produces.

If you go on Pinterest and search for Four Seasons pinners, you will find the major market hotels have accounts, each with a variety of boards with names that might surprise you — "Wicked Awesome Boston," "Rules We Live By," "Fashion Forward," "Summer Style Lookbook" and a "Just Because" board, to name a few. The content branches far from images of hotel grounds and golf courses, though those are also included, and empowers the audience with content they actually want to talk about. If you happen to be visiting any of these cities, you can easily find restaurants, local food and drinks to try, as well as what you might want to wear. About 50% of the content comes from the Four Seasons brand, which includes cocktails created from its menus and table decorations offered by its

You Get What You Give

wedding coordinators. The rest of the content, including all the furry little creatures in the "Just Because" board, are curated from various place on the Internet not associated with the Four Seasons brand.

Most impressively, the boards and pins use natural language. Four Seasons doesn't use robotic corporate talk in its descriptions of images or board names. Instead, the language is fun, interesting to read and offers a sense of discovery. When you see a Four Seasons pin in your home feed on Pinterest, you would not even notice it came from a company, but would probably think it came from one of your fellow pinners. A pin from Four Seasons might include a model dressed in trendy outerwear, as if clipped from a magazine, with a description of where to attain this fashionable item. Nothing about it says advertising or even "hotel."

It is the natural language and real human experience that helps drive Four Seasons' success on the platform. Four Seasons is using Pinterest the way its audience might use the platform. It's collected all the best of what it wants to keep and explore, then puts it up for display. The company does not seem worried about the intellectual property of its menus. It puts up content to build trust with its audience and positions the brand as an expert in areas of the industry. It gives real advice that its followers want and, in return, receives customer loyalty from the followers that enjoy its pins. Ultimately, when you travel to one of these

The Community Experience Strategy

cities and follow Four Seasons hotels, you will be more inclined to remember the Four Seasons name when planning your trip.

The company's health metric performance on the site is very good. Individual images are also getting decent engagement, with a number of repins and likes on each photo, which indicates that its audience really is using its content. Four Seasons is also consistent with its content, and keeps it up-to-date with new pins on boards every day. The brand is staying a part of the audience's everyday conversations, but with a supply of fresh ideas on a regular basis.

Posting consistently and with purpose is the key to all the strategies. The company has not let the content die off and has not left the account barren or unfinished.

The Community Strategy can exist on any social media platform but must represent the whole community and give the audience easy ways to mingle and communicate. Comments, chats, videos and images are all ways you can enrich the community experience. If possible, avoid censorship when it comes to your community's voice. The strong supporters in your community will oust naysayers if your brand is in good health. Publicly post your guidelines, rules and terms of engagement so that the community has a backbone to structure itself around. Most importantly, do not single out any micro-segments in your audience.

You Get What You Give

Endnotes

1 Chapman, C.C. "My Final Word on Ragu." Sept. 29, 2011.
http://www.cc-chapman.com/2011/my-final-word-on-ragu/.

2 Neisser, Drew. Fast Company, "Move Over Social Media; Here Comes Social Business." Sept. 23, 2011.
http://www.fastcompany.com/ 1779375/move-over-social-media-here-comes-social-business.

3 LinkedIn Marketing Solutions - EMEA, "Designing a social media strategy the IBM way." Dec. 13, 2012.
http://emea.marketing.linkedin.com/blog/designing-a-social-media-strategy-the-ibm-way/.

The Innovation Strategy

Sales may be plateauing, your design team may be out of fresh ideas, or your market may be saturated with copycat products. Your CEO is looking for new ways to grow market share and restart the fire that created your previously explosive sales, but you have no idea where to look. Luckily, you have a window to the immediate needs of your consumers. You have incredible access to a worldwide mindshare through social media that can evolve your products quickly and with purpose. You have smart consumers using your product, and advocates of your technology — no matter how simple or advanced — have their own ideas for improvement. If you give them the opportunity to participate with your business, the most passionate audience members will step up to the challenge and give back their ideas. Now is the time to harness your audience, show that you are open to smart changes, and, most importantly, show that you are ready to make those changes. These are the keys to the Innovation Strategy.

In the old school world of marketing, companies sent representatives to households to figure out why people were using products, how they were using them, and how those products integrated into their daily lives. A mind-boggling innovation from consumers led scent-maker Febreze to position itself differently and to rethink its marketing campaign. This innovation is what eventually led Febreze to reintroduce scents into its scent-eliminating formula.

The original formula for Febreze is designed to rid a room completely of any kind of odor. The product worked perfectly and exactly as designed. A big marketing budget was established to create commercials and get the genius product to fly off shelves. Yet, to marketers' surprise, Febreze was underselling at projected levels and sales were not increasing, but instead dropping! It was not until market researchers interviewed a woman with nine cats did they realize that people who live in stinky situations are accustomed to the harsh smells in their daily lives, and so have no reason to eliminate odors — an illustration of the problem at hand.[1] The initial idea in Febreze's marketing was to trigger the need for the product when people experienced

The Innovation Strategy

a bad smell. Thus, the spray of Febreze, which eliminated the smell, provided the reward of a clean scent. But that was all wrong. The trigger and reward loop was not working because humans adjust to their surroundings.

The marketers interviewed another woman. She used Febreze constantly and went through more bottles a month than they had initially estimated people would use. She was using the product as a way to finish a room. After she was done cleaning, she sprayed Febreze to "top off" the room. This made the marketers realize their trigger was misplaced. This woman was not using the product when she discovered a bad smell, but rather as a way to declare she was finished with the cleaning process. They redesigned the commercials to share a different trigger and reward loop: Enter a dirty room (the trigger), clean it, and then spray Febreze (the reward). With the new design of the trigger-reward loop, sales began to soar!

When Febreze was part of people's daily cleaning routines, not as an odor-eliminator but as a room finisher, fresh scents were the logical next innovation in the product line. Luckily for today's marketers, you don't have to travel across the country to get insights like these.

To implement the Innovation Strategy, you have to undoubtedly trust and believe in your audience. When putting the future of your brand or product in your audiences' hands, your brand needs to know that the audience can drive the company in the right direction. This also means that your audience must understand your brand. This ultimately means you have a strong brand and you have communicated your brand standards, position and vision to your audience well.

To effectively implement the Innovation Strategy, you will require a well-established and positive relationship with your consumers. This strategy can coincide well with a branding campaign or after your Community Experience Strategy takes hold. If your audience is not yet unified somewhere online, or you're not able to bring them together through other mediums like email or TV, then your first challenge will be to fix that issue. Then you can move on to innovating.

When considering this strategy, you must know exactly what you want to innovate and concentrate on a single aspect. Generating new products or doing a complete product overhaul is nearly impossible to implement correctly. Your consumers are not your product development team — they are your product improvement voice. They will work to generate ideas for you to make your product better, but will not fundamentally change your business. The conversation to prime your audience for this process should be as succinct and concise as possible. Focus on one particular element of the product you want to innovate and hold the forum around that. You must also be mindful that your audience online may only represent a segment of your total consumer market. While the majority of Americans are on social

The Innovation Strategy

media, many are lurking or are not active on a regular basis. Your innovation process also needs to be well-maintained and moderated.

The risk with this strategy is that the audience can overtake your channel. In July 2012, a microsite for Shell Oil Company was created to help innovate its marketing campaign. To celebrate its new Arctic drilling program, the microsite allowed users to generate their own images with the campaign slogan "Let's go," and then vote on which one was the best. It didn't take long for users to begin taking advantage of this generator to put out negative content such as "Birds are like sponges... for oil" and "Our oil is making the arctic a warmer, friendlier place, for us to get more oil." These images quickly spread across the Web and, in 24 hours, 1,500 tweets generated more than 2 million impressions, reaching an audience of 1.4 million people.[2]

An awful idea, right? Greenpeace thought so, too, and that's why it created the campaign as a spoof against Shell Oil Company.

The Shell brand was hijacked, as was the fake campaign, or at least that's what people who generated the hater content were led to believe they were doing. Greenpeace topped off the campaign with a fake Twitter account that threatened people who shared the images on Twitter with legal action. It was a complete mockery of the Shell brand. Although this campaign was a fake, it's a perfect worst-case scenario example of what could happen to your real campaign. If you are going to innovate, you must have a good brand presence, have the ability to moderate and trust your audience with this strategy. Don't give them something to hate.

When you get off on the right foot, your consumers will have a lot of ideas they want to see you make a reality. Before even opening the door to consumer input, make sure you outline exactly what you are looking for from them. Narrow down one feature of the product or one design aspect that you want to focus on, down to the most detailed points. For instance, if you want to innovate design, you want to make sure you are clarifying whether you are looking for aesthetic innovation or functional design. This will help you keep control of tangents and prevent you from losing your audience to scope creep in the innovation process.

Perhaps you are considering a new market. In this case, you want to make sure you talk to the audience in that market first. You can achieve this without alienation of any individuals in the community, but it requires clever pre-qualifications. You can use your channel to screen input and take the conversation of innovation into an offline channel, such as emails or phone calls, to continue the process with that particular audience. Social media is a great filter for the real world, and your audience is willing to exchange important demographic information for the right offer.

The best implementations of the Innovation Strategy are public and drive creativity within your audience. The process should create innovations for your brand and also build a stronger community. Innovation campaigns can double as word-of-mouth campaigns to drive awareness for your new innovation or product prelaunch. With this strategy, like all the others, you can gather vital information about your audience to help your marketing team understand your consumers better. You can gain a lot of knowledge about your customers if you give them the opportunity to be part of your brand's development. It is that kind of trust that builds the strongest relationships.

Master Your Industry

No matter what industry you are in, if your company is open to giving your consumers control and allowing them to help direct your products, the Innovation Strategy will work for you. Technology and software development companies are already doing this. Major social media platforms like Hootsuite and Wordpress are built on user requests and the slew of ideas that comes from the FAQ forums. It is their openness to user input and their ability to quickly implement innovations that got them to the top.

You Get What You Give

The number of submissions you receive can be daunting, as is the task of deciding which ideas to implement, and the order in which you implement them. Luckily, you have a few options in this arena. You can do a controlled release of new features, much like the way Facebook introduces new features to users in different locations around the world or based on platform usage. From there, you can get initial feedback for improvements and make necessary tweaks before releasing innovations to your whole audience. Twitter did the same thing with its redesign and business page release in December 2011.

There is an added side effect to limiting the release to segments of your audience; by doing this, you build a sense of scarcity, which builds anticipation in segments that did not get access. If you can maintain overall positive feedback on your controlled release and maintain good media connections, you can also gain an extra flurry of brand awareness.

Another option for organizing innovation submissions is to rank ideas of a similar type into a "top" list and then open the ideas to votes from your audience. Many software companies use this method when developing new features. Hootsuite, for instance, uses this method with a limited number of votes per person for specific feature requests, which adds a gaming element to the process. It forces the consumers to ask, "Which of these is most important to me?" By forcing that question upon your audience, you get the most thoughtful responses.

All feedback should be put against your product and brand goals as well. You do not want to develop features that change the fundamental direction of your business, no matter how many times they are requested.

There may be disagreements within your audience on which innovations are most important. This will test your abilities as a moderator. If you use a social media platform like Facebook or Twitter, where consumers can converse with each other openly, you will most likely find conflict. Have your innovation guidelines for posts and submissions at hand to refer to, and make sure your audience understands that conflict and hateful comments will not be tolerated. You can limit the type of interaction to simple voting by using custom-built Web applications, which eliminate any negativity in comments or responses. This, of course, requires a larger investment of resources.

Ben & Jerry's Flavor of Innovation

Ben and Jerry's realized its consumers can have better ideas than the people in the marketing department, and took full advantage of that fact. By creating an innovation website, the brand created a platform that leveraged millions of consumer ideas and brought them directly into the planning room.

You Get What You Give

Ben and Jerry's has been taking customer input for years. The company understood from the get-go that its consumers liked products more when they got to participate in creating them. It gave its audience a sense of ownership of the product. In 2010, it launched the "Do the World a Flavor" campaign, sporting a full-fledged ice cream-making "game" complete with instructional cows. It created a website platform it named the "Creation Station," where consumers could invent and name their own flavors of ice cream. Consumers were not strangers to the company's brand or voice and followed the brand down the path of tasty puns. Cherry Garcia, Chunky Monkey and Chubby Hubby were all flavors created by the devoted Ben and Jerry's audience. With this campaign alone, Ben and Jerry's generated 10,000 new flavor ideas.[3]

In June 2013, Ben and Jerry's introduced a twist on the flavor creation innovation in five major cities in the United States. Washington, D.C., New York, San Francisco, Portland and Seattle all had the opportunity to vote on specific aspects of ice cream for their respective cities. The final flavor was then introduced at big events later in the summer. Turnstiles were placed in the Williamsburg neighborhood in New York City for residents to vote on fair trade coffee or chocolate flavors. In Portland, bike lanes were divided into two sections. A rider could bike through different parts of the lanes to cast a vote for bananas or shortbread filling. In San Francisco, even the dogs got a vote; they could pick a flavor by drinking out of water bowls marked "chocolate" or "vanilla." Of course, anyone could go online and vote on the website, too. This flavor creation technique was a perfect mix of the real world and online experiences with a tasty payoff at the end.

Other food and beverage companies have also caught on to this trend. Mountain Dew, Vitaminwater, Dunkin' Donuts and many more have all jumped on the "create a flavor" bandwagon. It is a fairly simple and easy way to build awareness. Unfortunately, many of these companies did not go much farther than a simple awareness campaign and ignored the community opportunities the Innovation Strategy can bring.

Continuous Innovation

If you are going to implement the Innovation Strategy, you'll want to make sure it will last. This is not just a one-shot burst of brand awareness. You are building relationships with your audience during the entire process that offer leverage and advocacy that you will want to continue to build. A good campaign strategy is one that caters to continuous innovation and a revolving door of consumer experiences.

Mountain Dew and Vitaminwater both had the right ideas but let them flounder. Once a flavor was chosen and produced, it was rolled into the mix with the rest of the traditional and social content marketing that the other flavors received. What these companies missed out on was an opportunity to have audience innovators become true brand advocates. The innovation passed just as quickly as the excitement felt by the contest winners. The brands just let the campaigns fizzle out. What they could have done was use the leverage they created by having a contest to either create opportunities to collect more content and consumer information or to generate spin-off ideas.

Even two years after the official contest, Ben and Jerry's Creation Station is still up and running. The site explains the company is still "mulling over the flavor submissions," but its audience is more than welcome to continue to innovate. And why not? Ben and Jerry's put its time and effort into establishing the playground for its audience to be creative, so of course it should be open 24 hours! Whereas Mountain Dew and Vitaminwater have gone stale and closed the door on continuous engagement with their advocates, Ben and Jerry's has embraced its audience's potential and unlocked it. In many ways, it has cut out the competition. If consumers look for a particular flavor they wish existed, they know they can always go to the Creation Station and submit it. At least someone is listening!

Imagine if Vitaminwater had kept its flavor door open. It could have a database chalk-full of submissions and a constant flow of information from its audience. With a few clicks, it could find commonalities and develop new flavors that match new markets' tastes. In 2010, Vitaminwater, which is owned by Coca-Cola, lost 2.6% market share, while Sobe Lifewater, owned by PepsiCo, had just finished innovating its product and brand, and nearly doubled its market share.[4]

Your audience wants to know that you're listening. Even if the official contest is no longer open, you can keep the door open to continue the conversation and build those relationships with the people who really love your brand. You never know when an idea could spark your next product line. The Innovation Strategy is like having a 24/7 focus group with constant input for a relatively low investment.

Do Us A Flavor

Snack maker Frito-Lay also played the flavor game with consumers. In 2012 and early 2013, the company ran the "Do Us a Flavor™" campaign, which allowed users to submit flavors for Lay's potato chips that they wanted to see on shelves for a grand prize of $1 million. This contest was run through a microsite, Facebook, Twitter and text messages, where its audience could vote. Frito-Lay took entries through July 20, 2012, on the microsite and Facebook, and then had a celebrity panel, hosted

You Get What You Give

by Eva Longoria, choose the three flavor finalists out of 20 semi-finalists selected by the company.

The three flavors for consumers to choose from were Chicken & Waffles by Christina Abu-Jodum, Cheesy Garlic Bread by Karen Weber-Mendham, and Sriracha (a hot sauce) by Tyler Raineri. After being chosen, the flavors were produced by Frito Lay for Lay's lovers to purchase throughout February in stores, while the social media channels were opened to a nationwide vote.

The million-dollar prize undoubtedly motivated more than just Lay's lovers to submit entries; the contest yielded a total of 3.8 million submissions.[5] However, the winner was most definitely selected by true Lay's fans. Because the company went the extra step to actually produce these chips and drive its audience to buy, try and vote, it is likely that only the chip that truly tasted good to real Lay's lovers would win. Yes, friends and family of the contestants could have tried to sway the votes, but with the thousands of votes received for each flavor, it's unlikely the needle was significantly moved. Rather, the people willing to purchase the chips, follow the brand, and participate with Lay's were the ones to pull through for the company to select the winning chip flavor.

The campaign doubled as an enormous awareness campaign. Non-chip-eating or Lay's-loving consumers had a flood of "Do Us a Flavor" content in their streams. Even if you had not submitted, you may have been enticed to try the new flavor when it was out in February. It is difficult to measure, but it's likely that Frito-Lay acquired new consumers during the contest voting period, as well as increased sales among current fans. This is the genius behind the structure of the brand's use of the Innovation Strategy.

After a full month of voting, the winning chip turned out to be Karen Weber-Mendham's Cheesy Garlic Bread. This was the first "Do Us a Flavor" contest in the U.S., but not the first time Frito-Lay had held this type of contest. The company ran similar contests in England, India and South Africa. It harnessed its audience's collective palate to generate innovations like Walkie Talkie Chicken, Caesar Salad, Mastana Mango, Chili & Chocolate, and Cajun Squirrel. This goes to show that Frito-Lay has successfully innovated its product time and time again, which is key to the innovation strategy. This strategy requires an ongoing willingness to innovate with your audience, not just one-off campaigns.

The Innovation Game

Did you know the original Monopoly Game by Hasbro was released in 1934 and had a purse, lantern and a rocking horse as tokens? Those pieces were retired in 1950 and replaced by the

You Get What You Give

dog, man on horseback and wheelbarrow. Since 1950, the Howitzer, or cannon, and man on horseback have been retired. In 1999, the company introduced a competition for gamers to choose a new piece. Their choices were a piggy bank, biplane or a sack of money. The sack of money won and was put into the game through 2007.[6] This was one of the first instances where Hasbro showed trust in its audience to innovate its game.

Recently in 2012, the company set out for its next innovation, and again offered its audience the opportunity to choose the next game piece. But this time it was different. With more than 9 million fans on Facebook, Hasbro held its competition online and exclusively through Facebook. The first decision trusted with Monopoly fans was which current game piece should be saved. The company put up all its current game tokens and asked its audience to vote for their favorite. The least-popular token would be kicked out for good.

The campaign immediately began to get interesting. Although the campaign was for Monopoly, other brands began jumping on the contest to create teams to save pieces that resembled their products. Most notably, True Temper Tools created a series of "Save the Wheelbarrow" videos on YouTube to keep its piece of choice alive. These videos, which garnered thousands of views, depicted the wheelbarrow as a lifesaver in the most unusual circumstances. (Once it was used as a sink for dishwashing and once as a giant bowl for game day salsa.)

The Innovation Strategy

Online shoe and clothing retailer Zappos posted an image on Facebook in support of saving the shoe, and AAA tweeted images with the hashtag #teamracecar to save its beloved racecar token. In all, Scottie the dog raked in 29% of the votes to be saved, the racecar got 14% of the vote and the shoe and wheelbarrow came in with a narrow save of just over 8%. The iron was the odd one out and was relegated to the trash heap of history!

This was a big move by Hasbro, as it left the decision to remove game pieces in the hands of its fans. With the flurry of brands advocating for their pieces and users doing the same, the risks were high that a movement could be created to sabotage a specific piece. However, that was not the case. Monopoly was able to position itself as an even more iconic part of American culture and earned itself worldwide media attention and millions of impressions online. In the first month of 2013, Monopoly earned hundreds of headlines in newspapers and online publications nationally. Hasbro created leverage with its existing affinity for the game and made its contest into a national sensation with other brands' support.

Now, you may be asking, what token should replace the iron? A robot, guitar, cat, helicopter and diamond ring were put up for vote. If you know anything about the Internet, the final vote should be obvious (or at the very least, not surprise you). The contest ran through January 2013, and Monopoly fans from

You Get What You Give

185 countries voted to select the cat as the winner.[7] Depending on how you feel about the potentially misguided love the Internet holds for cats, this is where trusting its fans to innovate may have gone wrong for Monopoly. Nonetheless, Monopoly will distribute games with the new cat token later in 2013.

Endnotes

1 Cohan, Peter. Forbes, "Jurassic Park: How P&G Brought Febreze Back to Life." Last modified Feb. 19, 2012. http://www.forbes.com/sites/petercohan/2012/02/19/jurassic-park-how-pg-brought-febreze-back-to-life/2/.

2 Ward, Merlin U. "#ArcticReady a Frigid Fail." July 18, 2012. http://merlinuward.com/marketing/arcticready-a-frigid-fail.

3 Elliot, Amy-Mae. Mashable, "Power to the People: 3 Tasty Crowdsourcing Case Studies." Feb. 20, 2011. http://mashable.com/2011/02/20/crowdsourcing-case-studies/.

4 Stanford, Duane. Bloomberg Businessweek, "How PepsiCo Refreshed Its SoBe Water Brand." June 24, 2010. http://www.businessweek.com/magazine/content/10_27/b4185015651340.htm.

5 Kindlean, Katie. ABC News, "Lay's Cheesy Garlic Bread Potato Chips Win 'Do Us a Flavor' Contest." May 8, 2013. http://abcnews.go.com/blogs/lifestyle/2013/05/lays-cheesy-garlic-bread-potato-chips-win-do-us-a-flavor-contest/.

6 PR Newswire: Hasbro, Inc., "Voters Elect 'Sack of Money' as New Monopoly Game Piece." March 16, 2013. http://www.prnewswire.com/news-releases/voters-elect-sack-of-money-as-new-monopolyr-game-piece-75357812.html.

7 Truitt, Brian. USA Today, "'Monopoly' iron token is out, cat is in with fan vote." Feb. 6, 2013. http://www.usatoday.com/story/life/2013/02/06/new-monopoly-game-token/1895275/.

The Sales Strategy

This strategy was purposefully left for last because it seems intuitive that we want sales to result from our marketing efforts, especially on social media. After all, we are investing our time in this epic marketing channel for a return on investment. However, it was important that you read the previous strategies first, so you would understand the concepts and their applications. One other reason this strategy was left for last is that traditional sales tactics often are disruptive and too abrasive for social media. Brands that focus on pushing product through their social media channels often get tagged with the used car salesman stigma. Driving sales and having a sales strategy, however, is very different from that cheesy salesman approach. This strategy is best employed for the couponer and thrift-seeking audience.

The Sales Strategy uses a consumer's desire to stay on top of your latest offers to encourage participation on your channels and pass on incentives for purchasing. This strategy works primarily at the end of the purchase funnel. You will be focusing less on convincing people to become customers and more on upselling or selling to existing customers. The tactics used in this strategy work best for special and timely relaunches of products or new product introduction.

Fresh news and relevancy is key to the success of this strategy. You want to make sure your product or service has a reason for being plugged into a current conversation. Approaching this strategy with bullhorn tactics will only get you ignored. The "Glengarry Glen Ross"-style sales-or-death mentality will not succeed in social media. The one tactic that that can be taken from the traditional sales tactics and will do well in this strategy is friendliness.

If your brand is going to use social media strictly for sales, you will have to build that expectation from the beginning. If you already have a following, you will need to make a slow transition into it. If one day you are holding open conversations in a community environment and the next you are posting coupons and sales information, people will likely turn their backs on you or question you heavily about the sudden change.

A Time and Place

The worst thing you can do when it comes to the Sales Strategy is jumping into the wrong conversation. Context is everything with conversations, and you must make sure you understand the context of the conversation before you decide to join. Do three minutes of research before sending out messages to your audience, especially if you want to push out sales messaging, or you may end up biting your tongue.

On July 20, 2012, a mass shooting in a movie theater in Aurora, Colorado occurred during a screening for the *Dark Knight Rises*. Seventy people were wounded and 12 died that night. News of this horrific event spread across the United States through TV news, the Internet and newspapers. On Twitter, the hashtag #Aurora began trending and was featured prominently on Twitter's "trending topics" column. Then, the unthinkable happened. An online boutique, CelebrityBoutique.com, tweeted the following:

> *"#Aurora is trending, clearly about our Kim K inspired #Aurora dress ;-) shop: [link]"*

The backlash was immediate. The tweet was retweeted more than 650 times and online publishers picked up the story. People were outraged, calling for the marketing departments' heads.

You Get What You Give

This unfortunate tweet happened because the PR company that CelebrityBoutique.com had hired to handle the account failed to do its due diligence.[1] Had the company Googled "Aurora" or even clicked the hashtag to see what tweets were including it, they would have realized it was not a sales opportunity. If any response to the trending hashtag had to have been sent, it should have been one with empathy for the victims.

In February 2011, Cairo, Egypt, was in political upheaval. Riots were in the streets, and the country was in the international news spotlight. Kenneth Cole, a man with a brand all his own, tweeted the following:

> *"Millions are in an uproar in #Cairo. Rumor is they heard our new spring collection is now available online at [link] - KC"*

This tweet was amplified over 3,000 times by his following and people were upset. This tweet was no mistake, as KC sent it purposely and meant it to be humorous.[2] Nevertheless, backlash ensued and the public, his following and their following were upset. In reaction to the backlash, Kenneth Cole sent out an apology.

Your brand is being watched, whether it is by a few hundred people or a few thousand. Each member of your audience has his or her own following and it does not take long for one upset person to spread his or her feelings. Before you know it, you will have an angry mob with a voice that carries across multiple platforms, maybe even some on which you do not have a presence. Saying "sorry" does help, and it may slow or stop the hurt (go back and read the section titled "The Power of 'Sorry'" if you need a refresher), but when it comes to your online strategy, you should only be apologizing for inconveniencing your audience, not for insulting them or being insensitive.

Leading Consumers to Buy

When it comes to sales, there is one brand that really understands its audience. Best Buy is renowned for breaking its audience down to major "personas" (micro-segments) and even giving them names like "Jill," used to describe an upper-middle-class woman.[3] The brand has a psycho-graphic for every segment of shopper that walks through its doors. Although this may seem extreme, it plays a crucial role in how it presents its offers online. Best Buy can give each of its customer categories content that speaks to them specifically, and, in return, it gets happy customers who are more inclined to purchase and who remain dedicated to the brand.

Best Buy primarily posts its latest sales and promotions from its stores. It also crowd-sources sales offers with its audience members by asking them to vote on which items in the store should be on sale through their Facebook page. Take a look at the company's Facebook wall and see the tactics in action. The majority of posts include a link to the product depicted. Each post drives hundreds, sometimes thousands, of people to the website — and they post multiple times a day.

Best Buy has made a distinct choice in what it does not want to share online. You will not see publicized product reviews, instructional videos on products or community-generated content. It only posts content that features specific products or categories of products. Every now and then you will find a YouTube video of one of its commercials.

Most impressively, Best Buy has a knack for keeping its posts relevant, in that it also makes references to pop culture. On Groundhog Day 2012, Best Buy made three major posts with references to *Groundhog Day* the movie, starring Bill Murray. On June 10, 2013, with announcement of the new Xbox One console, Best Buy posted a simple status update with a link to preregister the new tech. Despite not including an image or link preview, this post drove 9,800 people directly from the Facebook page to the Xbox One landing page.

All of its tactics are designed to inform its audience of the deals and sales in a friendly and happy way. Its focus is on happy shopping through its social media, and it keeps its audience engaged with its sales with a focus on specific mindsets. It creates a sense of urgency and excitement around its offerings, rarely with the call to action to "Buy now!" The audience has come to expect the latest information on product sales.

Fashion Success

Just a year after Foursquare was launched, a clever brand jumped on the geo-location opportunity to drive awareness and sales for a new sneaker. New product launches can be difficult and expensive, and high-end fashion brand Jimmy Choo was looking for a simple but effective solution. It realized that a lot of people were talking about its brand on social media, but wanted to get what was being said online to spread offline as well. Working off the insight that much of its marketing relied on word of mouth, Jimmy Choo created a campaign that took advantage of social media's massive reach and encouraged offline conversation.

Jimmy Choo created "CatchAChoo" accounts on Foursquare, Twitter and Facebook.[4] Its audience was asked to follow one of the accounts and wait for the chance to find and win a pair of the new sneakers. A representative of Jimmy Choo would "check in" at a location and wait for a few minutes. Through Foursquare, Jimmy Choo pushed check-in notifications to the "CatchAChoo" Facebook and Twitter accounts. Whoever saw the notification, found the representative and said, "I'm following you" first, ended up with the new pair of sneaks.

Jimmy Choo went into this campaign with two goals: to raise awareness of the new sneaker and to generate sales. By using the new platform Foursquare as the center of its strategy, the company was also able to generate earned media. Four weeks and 134 check-ins later, the campaign was a success. Jimmy Choo reported a 33% increase in sales of the new sneakers, 4,000 mentions on Twitter alone and a 40% increase in positive mentions of the brand.[5]

More Than Money

The traditional definition of a sale is the exchange of a commodity (or item) for money. Businesses use that earned money to obtain resources to produce more items to sell. But what if you could skip the money part and obtain the resources directly? That is what Sport Club do Recife set out to do.

Sport Club do Recife is a soccer fan club from the city of Recife, Brazil. Brazil has some of the most passionate soccer fans in the world and there are hundreds of thousands of them. Brazil also had an organ transplant shortage. Transplant organs are an incredibly valuable resource, but organs cannot currently be bought or manufactured. (People are fond of their organs and

The Sales Strategy

tend to want to hold on to them for as long as possible.) But mix in the avid passion of a sports club, and you have a recipe for a movement that can shift the status quo.

With the leverage of more than 100,000 of Sport Club do Recife's members and their passion for the game, the "Immortal Fans" campaign was launched. This campaign rested on the culture of the Sport Club do Recife, which binds members together like life-long friends. The members are fanatical, some putting the team before family. The crux of the "Immortal Fan" was that, even after death, a sport club member could live on, helping another member live to support the team, have the lungs to shout at the competition, and have the eyes to watch the team win.

Harnessing the members' passion, the sport club recruited members through its Facebook fan page to become registered organ donors with the promise of perpetuating the club's fandom. The club increased Brazil's organ donation rate by 54% in one year — a new record. A series of videos from organ donors was created to share the promise that donors make to the club and to organ recipients. In a short period of time, more than 51,000 club members signed up to become donors.[6] Brazil and the Sport Club do Recife sold their devoted audience the opportunity to live forever with the "Immortal Fan" program and got one of the most valuable resources in the world in return.

You Get What You Give

The challenge for your sales strategy is to have continuous growth and keep your campaign current. One company has been running the same strategy since 2006, just one year after the launch of YouTube. Blendtec produces a $400 version of a kitchen staple and was having difficulty increasing sales. It knew it had a powerful product, but it was difficult to create that sense of worth through its website. Enter "Will It Blend," a campaign that might be the most memorable and longest-running sales strategy on social media.

Blendtec marketing director George Wright witnessed CEO Tom Dickson testing the Blendtec blender's toughness by shoving pieces of wood into it. This gave him the idea to demonstrate the toughness of the blender to the world. With a very small budget, the marketing team recorded five videos of Dickson blending odd objects. The first video, in which Dickson blended marbles, garnered more than 23,000 views on the first day. Realizing the instant success of these videos, the company continued to put out videos, with Dickson blending everything from a garden rake to glow sticks to a golf club. By the fourth year, the company reported a 700% increase in retail sales, but it didn't stop there.[7] After more than 100 videos and some gross blends like the "cochicken" — a Coke and half a rotisserie chicken — the company continues to keep its "Will It Blend" objects current. Tom Dickson has blended iPhones, iPads, current video games and even made references to the 2012

Mayan apocalypse calendar when he tried to blend a Blendtec blender with a Blendtec blender. Albeit cheesy with an intro akin to that of *The Price Is Right*, complete with blinking marquee lights, the company has consistently engaged its audience and proved the value of its $400 blender.

Sales are not impossible to achieve and measure with social media. The old return on investment formula can be applied — whether the return is an improvement from other marketing channels is another story. However, social media is one of the only channels that can actually give you a lot more than just monetary exchange from your investment. It is a connection builder. When used to its fullest potential, it builds real emotional connections between your brand and your consumers that go well beyond the ROI formula.

You Get What You Give

Endnotes

1 Olanoff, Drew. TNW News, "Celeb Boutique – You Freaking Morons." June 20, 2012. http://thenextweb.com/socialmedia/2012/07/20/celeb-boutique-you-freaking-morons/.

2 Sweet, Ken. CNN Money, "Kenneth Cole Egypt tweets ignite firestorm." Feb. 4, 2011. http://money.cnn.com/2011/02/03/news/companies/KennethCole_twitter/.

3 White, Brian. DailyFinance, "Best Buy internal demographics training manual leaked." March 19, 2008. http://www.bloggingstocks.com/ 2008/03/19/best-buy-internal-demographics-training-manual-leaked/.

4 On a side note: The company used a Facebook personal profile for this promotion, which violates current Facebook terms of use, and is not recommended for strategies today.

5 InsideFMM, "Case Study: Jimmy Choo Foursquare Campaign." May 27, 2010. http://insidefmm.com/2010/05/catchachoo-jimmy-choo-foursquare-campaign/.

6 "Immortal Fans" Recorded May 24 2013. Ogilvy Brazil. Web, http://www.youtube.com/watch?v=-8GFcAlWhBM.

7 "Blendtec Case Study." http://www.freebusinessvideosri.com/uploads/6/1/1/4/6114711/blendteccasestudy.pdf.

Real-time Marketing

Real-time marketing is the latest trend in online marketing. It is the evolution of the traditional method of using CRM software and analytics. It aims to give you immediate insights from your customers' behaviors online in real time. Armed with this information, you can adjust your marketing, messaging, and content on the fly to engage your customers in the most appropriate way for that instant in time.

Data flows through the Internet at lightning speeds. Thousands of people join social networks daily and are putting more personal information online than ever before. The amount of content going online daily would take you a lifetime to sift through manually. Just managing the information coming in from your channels can be daunting, and that's not including the information floating around your industry, competitors and potential customers — all of which you should also be monitoring. Truth be told, brands are just as inundated with information as their audiences.

The opportunity in all this data floating around is that you can be more informed. In a split second's notice, you can make your marketing more effective for each micro-segment. This data flow could include location information, personal information and business information. "Location data" includes information such as weather, climate, traffic or live events. "Personal information" includes your audience's conversation topics, sentiments, and interests. "Business data" includes information such as the type of customer — whether its your customer or your competitor's customer — how much she spends, or where she is in the purchase cycle. A full scope of information and the commonalities between these data points enable you to keep your finger on the pulse of what your audience is doing, how they feel and whether it is the right time to make the ask to purchase.

You may have heard the term "big data" — this is what we are talking about. It is best to think of "big" not as "large amounts," but rather "big decisions" or "important decisions." There may be a lot of data, but when synthesized and presented correctly and with a good execution plan, you will have a clear picture of the next steps you need to take based on the output. The tools mentioned in the Basic Social Media Strategy chapter have parts of real-time marketing built into them, but you can also do some real-time marketing through manually monitoring specific channels. If you have already researched where your customers get their information on products, you should also be watching those spaces to stay up-to-date. Use Facebook Graph Search, Google Plus Trends and Twitter Search to monitor keywords related to your business. Knowing what your customers are talking about and what they are sharing is a big part of the real-time marketing process. To take full advantage of real-time marketing, it is recommended that you invest in a tool that monitors multiple categories of information and builds actionable data for you.

Automation

You may be tempted to make sweeping generalizations about your audience and set up automated or cookie-cutter responses to people using specific keywords in their conversations. Cutting corners to skip the analysis and synthesis of marketing data will hurt your brand in both the short and long run. Automation on the Internet is a big fat no-no. An automated response is tantamount to a form letter and should be avoided. Nothing is more disruptive to the social media environment than blatantly automated responses. Using automation with any of these strategies puts you at risk of producing content that may seem relevant on the surface, but is seriously out of place. You are risking your brand's integrity. When one person suspects an automated response — especially other marketers — he will look a little deeper and it won't be difficult to discover your secret. That person may share your secret and post it on the Web, or just block your account. It is a risk you do not want to take.

There are services that allow you to manage thousands of potential followers with a variable tweets generated based on boilerplates. It is a catchy idea and sometimes successful, but because it is not human, it can miss the context of the content and create a negative reaction. This small margin of error may not seem bad, until people start talking about it and it becomes a viral disaster.

Some companies use these services, and almost all of their tweets are automated through a system. These kinds of tweets tend to employ old sales tactics. These brands are jumping into conversations with a sales agenda and almost zero understanding of consumer need or relationship-building. Even Alec Baldwin's character from *Glengarry Glen Ross*, Black the sales legend, would scoff at these tactics. They are selling people who haven't even walked on the lot.

It is not difficult to catch automation. A dead giveaway is the small variability in outgoing tweets and the frequency in which they are produced. Do not become an automated bullhorn and ignore the opportunity for conversation. Social media is not a push channel: it's a "get what you give" channel. If you are not giving value, you won't get any. Including a link to your website in every message may get a few clicks, but unless you have a relationship with your audience you won't get much further than the people who have opted into your feeds. Your audience will not share your content on your behalf, and most likely will lose interest in your promotional behavior over time.

Fine-Tuning

Now that you have read about all five strategies and where social media marketing is going in the near future, you are prepared to create a better social media presence. While each of these case studies have their own twists, turns and special considerations, they represent brands that have made the strategies work for them. Each company must use these strategies for its own purposes and rely on the values, goals, processes and abilities of their company and staff to make the strategies work best for them. There is no blanket answer to a social media problem that will solve all business problems across the board. Each business is unique — and that's a good thing! The more unique you can be, the better audience you can build around that uniqueness. Just remember that you will encounter challenges, but so will everyone else.

Marketing takes a lot of work. The old days of pushing out ads to influence purchase intent do not work in this noisy world. Marketing must be laser-focused and, lucky for you, social media gives you that ability. The information available about your customers, your competitors' customers and anyone else can help you be more effective when you use it correctly. You have a great opportunity to map out your customers on a micro-segment, and an individual basis. You can understand them, their needs, interests and even aspirations. Using this information, your brand can support your audience, help them succeed where they want to succeed and build real relationships with them.

It's not enough to have awareness. You need connections. These connections and relationships will drive your brand farther than you can imagine.

Allow your brand to give its all and you will get it back. People are not robots; they want belonging and they want to reciprocate good feelings. That is the value at the core of the "you get what you give" principles. Let the bad apples rot and your shining stars light up the sky!

Your brand can use these five strategies on any channel you deem fit. They are all very different and require different tactics. Some of these tactics may overlap, and that is what gives your social presence continuity. That gives the people who follow your brand in multiple places the same tone and brand voice throughout your social presence.

Mixed Strategies

"But wait, there's more!"

Yes, there is a major caveat to the five social media strategies. By now you have realized that you probably will not be employing just one strategy on any single platform. You may have multiple platforms using different strategies, but you may also use two strategies on one platform. The secondary strategy is usually a derivative of the audience engagement. Your audience may not require a full pivot to a different strategy, but rather will have a micro-segment that falls under a different strategy and requires a different approach or type of engagement.

You will find that one strategy will work best for most your audience on a platform, but a portion of them will also want different information.

For instance, your Community Experience Strategy may have also garnered a group of passionate innovators. Within your community, you now also have a circle of people sharing innovation ideas with you. You will have to acknowledge this crowd in an effort to make them feel included. If your brand is open to innovation, you may even consider employing the Innovation Strategy in conjunction to the primary Community Experience Strategy. You can develop content that targets the innovators specifically while maintaining a rich community.

Similarly, you may also find that rewarding your community with coupons and discounts for participation helps drive sales. These strategies are flexible that way.

The challenge with mixed strategies is making sure that your metrics align across strategies. This overlap in your business metrics can be effective, but make sure that your activities from combined strategies are driving related business metrics.

A few brands do this very well. Both Expedia and Hotwire use their Twitter accounts for a mixed strategy of community and sales. They have grown a community of passionate travelers and therefore share information on the best destinations, travel tips and consumer-generated content. They bask in their communities' passion for travel and adventure. The trust they have built with their audience brought forth the opportunity to enhance the travel experiences of the people they converse with by presenting travel deals and sales. This tactic is a natural fit for their content. It is also well-received by their audiences.

Finding that perfect mix is always a challenge. There is no magic ratio of sales-to-community post updates that will drive every business the same way. It is all based on what you hear from your community. If you are tracking your content, you will gain insights that optimize your content. The feedback you get on any post and the engagement metrics you track will help you to push your strategies further along.

You must listen to the needs of your audience and fulfill those needs. Any of the five strategies can be paired together, depending on what your audience wants and on which channels you decided to create a presence.

Multi-brand vs. Single Brand

Major conglomerates and brands with multiple physical locations face unique issues. You have probably asked yourself, "Do I create one page for all products or multiple pages for each product?" The pro to having unique profiles for all your brands under one umbrella is simplicity. On the downside is the challenge of physically managing all those different presences. Before deciding to create unique profiles for all your brands, you must first consider whether your brands have the same audience. If your company can afford multiple community managers and creative designers, a presence for individual brands may be right for you.

On the other hand, if your brands are very similar, or are iterations of a core product, keeping your brands under an umbrella profile is recommended. The key is to balance the management and content creation time with the results you want for each brand. Consider whether the voice of each brand could be used when combined together. Also consider if goals for each brand could be accomplished under one umbrella.

Coca-Cola boasts 3,500 beverages under 500 different brands, 1,000 of which are juices, and many of them have their own divisions of labor. More than 3% of all beverages consumed worldwide are Coke products.[1] However, you don't see a Mountain Dew post on the Coca-Cola brand pages. Not all Coke drinkers are Mountain Dew drinkers. If you could take a peek at the demographic analysis, you would see the audiences for Coke and Mountain Dew are very different. Just by comparing the individual advertisements, you can see there is a distinct difference in tone, voice and branding. Almost all of Coke's brands have their own social media channels, most of them using a Community Experience Strategy.

You may not have as many brands as Coca-Cola, but the same principles apply. If you feel you have a lead product, then feature it as your flagship. Consider whether your other products are complementary and can be wrapped up into the same channel as supporting products and content. If the other brands would create confusion, noise, or disrupt the flow of your strategy, you may require a separate social brand identity.

Kroger has kept everything under the same umbrella. Using the Sales and Community Experience Strategies, it updates its audience with information on how to find its products at its major distributors.

You Get What You Give

Choice Hotels has 11 different brands, all of which are maintained under a single, official "Choice Hotels" presence on each channel. Although many of their individual locations have profiles of their own, they are not well-managed. The company has not allocated resources to manage all these locations. They could consider consolidating their locations under individual brand umbrellas at the very least, or could concentrate all brand activities under the Choice Hotels page.

Kraft, on the other hand, has separate Facebook pages for its famous Kraft Singles, Kraft Mac N' Cheese and Kraft Dressing, but has a "Kraft Foods" Facebook page as a single page for its audience to discover recipes and cooking tips with other Kraft brands.

The choice is yours. Do your brands have large enough audiences and a sufficiently unique brand voice to warrant their own channels?

Endnotes

1 Bhasin, Kim. Business Insider Australia, "15 Facts About Coca-Cola That Will Blow Your Mind." June 10, 2011.
http://www.businessinsider.com.au/facts-about-coca-cola-2011-6.

Preparing for Tomorrow

The possibilities and innovations with social media are only limited by the technology available. New opportunities are arriving every year on the Internet in the form of new platforms, applications and ever-increasing connectivity of consumers. More of the world is gaining access to the Internet, joining social networks and starting new conversations every day.

As marketers, our challenge is to become part of those conversations in a meaningful ways. We must seek out and pursue opportunities that add value to our audience's daily lives. We shouldn't ignore the interests of our businesses, but those interests also should not be at the forefront of our social media agendas. We need to be interested in our audience and also be interesting ourselves. Act with human qualities and with human interests that give a sense of connection and belonging. The audience comes first; the message comes second. The relationships that we build with our audiences will eventually help us realize our business goals. This will take time, but the long-term value of having a trusting audience with a natural affinity for the brand is worth the effort and energy.

When it makes sense, our brand should join the individuals in our audience as they explore new mediums and technology. There are advantages to being the first movers on networks that have just launched. General Electric and Lowe's jumped onto Vine with entertaining and meaningful content. General Electric created interesting six-second looping videos on technology and science, while Lowe's provided home improvement tips in their videos. Although Vine was not yet at a critical mass of users, and followers of the brand may not have even joined the platform yet, the content the brands created could be repurposed on other channels. The presence they had also gave them leverage for earned media.

The future of social media may not be technologies with explosive growth like Facebook, Twitter or Pinterest. Nevertheless, having that presence with a strategy that puts the audience first and being part of the audiences' exploration will build awareness.

You may discover new markets by staying on top of what is coming next. Social media is led by technology, and technology developers and designers are getting smarter about how they create their products. They too are aware that the average consumer is inundated with messages from all directions. To get their technologies off the ground, they don't just have to focus on a specific problem to solve, but often have to focus on a specific person or micro-segment for that problem. Hyper-specialized apps, networks and tech are being developed each year.

What Apple said in its advertisements is true: "There's an app for that." You want to track your pregnancy on a daily basis to get the perfect picture, and then create a 1-minute time-lapse video? There's an app for that! It's called CineMama.

But that is all that app does. There is a different app for tracking menstrual cycles for when you are trying to get pregnant, and yet another for pregnancy dieting. Pick any topic and there are at least three apps, all with different angles, on how to solve a specific problem for a specific person. Stay on top of these trends and the technology being developed around certain markets and you may find yourself a with very unique, precise target market for your current or next product.

On the other end of the spectrum, you can use technology to drive your business. CineMama was actually developed by the March of Dimes Foundation as a way to build awareness for its cause. It's not a technology company, but it recognized that this app was needed and could also be a marketing tool. It gave women a way to have a better experience with their pregnancies, and expecting mothers rejoiced. March of Dimes, in return, gets support for its cause and its message gains access in places it might not otherwise have been able to reach.

Chipotle has also jumped on this trend and recently created a video game where your character, a scarecrow, fights against big, mass-production food companies in an effort to promote better food and healthier eating. Customers who complete the game earn a buy one, get one free offer at the restaurant. All this supports its marketing campaign for fresh ingredients.

These examples are the epitome of "you get what you give." By fulfilling an unrelated need of their audience through content, games, or apps, brands earn permission to send out their message in a covert, inoffensive way while building stronger relationships with their audiences.

Wherever you decide to participate with your audience, you must understand the environment and the potential pitfalls of your actions. You have the potential to accelerate your brand online, but it can just as easily go spiraling out of control. While implementing these strategies, you should use tactics that impact the personal lives of your audience but do not disrupt the behavior norms with network faux pas or taboos. Do your research on the best practices of each network before jumping in and posting.

Your audience is your most powerful asset. You may want to give them a cause to rally behind. You may crowd-source their thoughts and share them across your following or implement them internally. You may want to enhance experiences they are already enjoying with your brand through engagement and interaction.

No matter your strategy, a well-managed audience will build meaningful relationships between individuals and your brand. As your knowledge grows about your audience and your platforms, your strategies will evolve. You will find which mix of content best engages your audience but still meets your business goals.

Social media is not instant gratification. Building your audience will take time. And it won't just be days, but rather months or even years before you become a sizable force in the social media realm. It takes the same amount of time to build online relationships with your audience members as it would to do it in person. The advantage to social media is that it is scalable. You can build relationships and have concurrent conversations with multiple people at the same time. Just like in real life, there may be some people who are not interested or are not interesting to your brand, and, just like in real life, you can go your separate ways with a mutual understanding of your surface-level relationship. There also will be people who are very interested in your brand, products and service. Engage with them, support them and in time you may transform them into evangelists for your brand.

You Get What You Give

Some of your channels may grow faster than others. The channels that are more conversational typically give you leverage to increase your following quickly because you can have an exchange directly with members of your audience without them having to engage with the content you put out first. You will face the temptation to abuse that direct channel by pushing unwanted content to them. Resist that temptation. Just because you *can* message an individual directly doesn't mean you *should* bombard them with your brand messages. If you feel this urge coming over you, take a step back and think about the engagement from your recipients' point of view. Then ask yourself if you are really adding value to their stream and driving the right reactions with the access they give you to their feed by opting to follow you. If the content comes off abrasive, try something else.

Social media is, first and foremost, social. Give your audience content they want or need more often than pushing out content that fulfills your needs. No one likes that friend who always talks about him or herself.

Be wary of the "health metrics" in social media. These metrics do not drive your business and are milestones at the most. Your social actions should be connected to "business metrics" that drive your business by either minimizing a cost or increasing brand value or revenue. Take the time before pushing out content to consider what actions and business metrics you want to impact with social media. Get a baseline value for your current activities and test new content and engagement tactics to improve these metrics.

Each interaction you have with an audience member can be measured and, at the very least, correlated to a business metric. There are a number of tools available that can measure every move of your social activity, from the number of engagements with your content to trends in account growth and post optimization. You can measure social impact on anything from sales, purchase intent, brand awareness, referrals, and even customer turnover.

As marketers, we have to set the expectation for consumers online. The world is raising a "social media society," one that feels entitled to free stuff, whose tastes change more rapidly than ever before and whose attention spans are diminishing to mere seconds. Your audience is inundated with a constant stream of information from friends, and, as more analog mediums like TV move online, there will be even more content bombarding them.

We must do more than just be in front of our audience. We must engage them. We must learn about them. We must care about them. Take into account the individual interests of your audience and the insights you might glean from that knowledge that drives your business. Show them you are listening, and that, as a brand, you are there to help fulfill a need that they have. Give them the reason they should follow you. Build a

You Get What You Give

relationship with the individuals in your audience based on the fact that you will not abuse their willingness to opt in to your content, but will instead entertain, inspire and empower them.

There is only one concept you must remember above all else: You get what you give.

Note to the Reader

Thank you for reading this book. I know that there are many things you could have done with the time you spent reading, and I hope, as any author would, that you enjoyed the concepts and stories within these pages. My goal with this book is to help community managers, their supervisors, and their clients understand the value in social media, as well as the ways to show that value. While this book focuses on the fundamentals, I plan on writing more on individual concepts, such as attribution of social media to business activities, in-depth metrics, and tools for effective execution of social media strategies. Also, if there are any particular sections of this book you would like to see expanded, please let me know.

If you enjoyed reading this book, in addition to recommending it to others (nudge, nudge), I recommend a number of other books that can help you:

- "Predictably Irrational" by Dan Ariely — As marketing focuses more and more on behaviors, Ariely's book provides a glimpse into peoples' irrational behaviors and how we can predict these behaviors. I see great application of this book in your short- and long-term marketing. At the very least, it is an entertaining read.
- "All Marketers are Liars" by Seth Godin — Despite being published in 2005, the ideas in this book are timeless. Godin explores the art of storytelling and understanding your consumer in ways you might not have ever considered.
- "Great by Choice" by Jim Collins and Morten T. Hansen — The sequel to "From Good to Great," this book builds on the concepts and dives deeper into the leadership and cultures that make great companies. It is not a marketing book, but it has great information on how to build business processes and has wonderful ideas on company culture.

Until we get a chance to meet in person, or until the next book comes out, I will continue to blog and will be available on my social media channels. I invite and encourage you to reach out to me with any questions you have about your marketing programs or those that you see online. As the social media landscape continues to grow, shift, and evolve, I too will have new questions that need answers. Together, we can work to find those answers.

Finally, I would like to show my gratitude to you for taking the time to read this book. Send an email to me at MerlinUWard@gmail.com with "You Get What You Give" in the subject line, and I will send you a link to download an eBook I have co-authored for free.

Thank you!

About the Author

Merlin U Ward comes from an entrepreneurial background. After successfully launching his first business at 18, he found his knack for business processes and marketing. He adopted the philosophy "marketing is a part of everything," where marketing is approached as a part of every business process, from product development to accounts receivable. It is from this philosophy and his years consulting businesses in Arizona that Merlin fell in love with the diverse applications of social media.

As social media evolved, Merlin continued to explore the new networks and tools that came along with the changing landscape. Merlin joined Renegade, an agile social media agency in New York City, in 2012. As Renegade's social media strategist, he applied and enhanced processes for implementing, tracking, and improving companies' social media presences.

Merlin continues to explore and develop frameworks for marketing, social media and social media analytics. He is a proponent of building better business and doing better marketing through better understanding of your customers.

In his free time Merlin brews his own beer and travels with his wife. You'll find him in the mix enjoying a craft beer and wearing funky socks!

Twitter: @MerlinUWard
LinkedIn: in/MerlinUWard
Instagram: @MerlinUWard

www.ingramcontent.com/pod-product-compliance
Lightning Source LLC
Chambersburg PA
CBHW071759200526
45167CB00017B/502